Monica,

My daughter from
another mother.

THE
PENDULUM

I love you to life

Honit !

THE
PENDULUM
COME BACK SWINGING THROUGH THE DIFFICULT TIMES

RICKIE G. RUSH

DESTINY IMAGE® PUBLISHERS, INC.

P.O. Box 310, Shippensburg, PA 17257-0310

"Promoting Inspired Lives."

This book and all other Destiny Image, Destiny Image Fiction books are available at Christian bookstores and distributors worldwide.

Cover design by: River Publishing & Media Ltd.

For more information on foreign distributors, call 717-532-3040.

Reach us on the Internet: www.destinyimage.com.

ISBN 13 TP: 978-0-7684-0467-8

ISBN 13 Ebook: 978-0-7684-0468-5

For Worldwide Distribution, Printed in the U.S.A.
1 2 3 4 5 6 7 8 / 18 17 16 15 14

DEDICATION

One day when I was supposed to be working on a title for this book, I found myself picturing my brother, Anthony, his body rife with pain, in his favorite position—down on his knees, seeking God's face.

Anthony, who'd been diagnosed with lung cancer, taught us all how to come back swinging after being knocked down. Through the initial diagnosis, a lung transplant, and rounds and rounds of radiation and chemotherapy, Anthony continued to fight through to his ultimate, victorious recovery. The day he died, my sister-in-law found him (once again) in his favorite position, kneeling alongside their bed, spending critical time with God.

I watched Anthony use prayer and his faith to free himself from the excessive heaviness of the oncologist's bad report. When he was so physically exhausted from being poked and prodded, needled and nudged, he tapped into his unwavering faith as an energy source, so he could muster up enough strength to swing those arms like a champion boxer, who in spite of having lost all the previous rounds, was still swinging his way through the very last round of a championship match.

We cannot allow the difficult times to cause us to get stuck. Instead, we are all called to be "Anthonys." Brother, this one is for you—one of the best champions to ever live.

ACKNOWLEDGMENTS

When God gives us a vision, it's never His intention that we accomplish it alone. The right people come at the right time, and the right circumstances emerge from mistakes that seem irreparable.

To *Bishop T.D. Jakes* for his encouragement and inspiration in sharing this vision and taking a risk,

To my editor, *Jackie Macgirvin* at Christianbookdoctor.com, who kept my nose to the grindstone,

To *spiritual* and *natural family members* and *friends* who stood behind me and pushed when I wanted to stop moving forward,

To powerful *leaders* (including *Pastor Harry Lee Sewell*) who have inspired other leaders to come back swinging,

To *principals, teachers,* and *educators* who teach others to seek excellence and not perfection,

To *coaches* who know the limitations of their players and still put them in the game,

To the *doctors, nurses,* and *medical professionals* who wouldn't let me give up,

To my *classmates* and *childhood friends* who helped motivate me to strive for success,

To members of the *"Machine"* whose faith in my story brought me to this destination,

To *graduates* at every level of completion who are stepping into a new beginning,

To *politicians* and *business professionals* who work for the good of others without always seeing the benefit,

To *everyone* who endured through my setbacks and celebrated my comebacks,

Thank you. This book is our shared victory.

To everything there is a season,
A time for every purpose under heaven:
A time to be born,
And a time to die;
A time to plant,
And a time to pluck what is planted;
A time to kill,
And a time to heal;
A time to break down,
And a time to build up;
A time to weep,
And a time to laugh;
A time to mourn,
And a time to dance;
—ECCLESIASTES 3:1-4, NKJV

CONTENTS

FOREWORD

Many Christians think they are not free to express their emotions or feelings if they are the least bit negative. But as human beings made by God, He knows our every strength and weakness—and loves us anyway. You must have faith that God knows you and loves you, no matter what you are going through or feeling.

In my sermon *The Fight with Frustration*, I speak about how God draws the best out of people. He knows you from the inside out because His Holy Spirit lives within you; therefore, He allows (sometimes uncomfortable and sometimes downright scary) worldly situations to help mold godly character. He allows experiences to infiltrate your mind and body that may surprise and challenge you. For instance, Moses faithfully led his people from slavery toward the Promised Land—and the people complained. Job faced terrible losses including his children, property, and livestock—and his wife told him to curse God, and his friends were of no comfort at all. What is a good Christian person to do during these times?

In *The Pendulum,* Pastor Rickie Rush brings home the reality of life's inevitable frustrating circumstances that cause people—yes, even Christians—to become depressed and downtrodden. He gives you answers to questions that have been haunting you in the dark and keep you wondering in the light of day. You will learn how to handle downtimes and realize that throughout the seasons of life there swings a pendulum back and forth, carrying with it good and bad, happy and sad.

God's grace is sufficient to guide you through anything the devil throws at you—every day and in every way, until He calls you to your eternal home with Him. Until then, you can rise up swinging through every difficult time.

BISHOP T.D. JAKES
Founder, The Potter's House
Dallas, Texas

INTRODUCTION

Out of all the topics a pastor could write about, you're probably wondering why in the world I would choose to tell people how to defeat the enemy by coming back swinging *through difficult times.*

Well, I actually did consider writing about *building a strong marriage or how to be a good steward of your finances,* but when I thought about all the issues that my church members encounter over and over, it was clear to me that God's people needed to know how to handle difficult times. This topic was the common thread that sewed together our patchwork quilt of tragedies and triumphs.

I was constantly telling people that everyone gets discouraged, tripped up, counted out, and pushed or knocked down. But not everyone gets up; and I found myself fascinated by those who did. I was curious about the difference between the two groups, particularly since I spent far more time teaching, coaching, mentoring, and encouraging those who were down.

I noticed that the group who chose to stay down had several problems:

- Most had only heard *part* of God's message regarding satan and his attacks. They seemed to exist solely on "bits and pieces."

- Often, they had been knocked down by some loss or disappointment and had placed the blame squarely on God's shoulders.

- Many seemed stuck; their clocks, if you will, had simply stopped ticking. They had made pit stops along some of the same dead-end roads I myself had traveled: Bitterness Avenue, Grief Street, Anger Road, etc.

So, after 44 years of being an evangelist, pastoring for 24 years, and as someone who had faced his own share of knock-downs, I knew exactly what topic God had called me to cover in this book.

Christians are engaged in spiritual warfare against our enemy, satan, who prowls around like a roaring lion trying to devour each and every one of us (see 1 Peter 5:8). As much as we desire to know about God and His plan for our lives, we need to know just as much about satan, his purpose, and his plan for our lives.

If you weren't in a difficult season, you probably wouldn't have picked up this book. I want to encourage you that as Christians we *are* the victors. And you hold in your hand the tools that can teach you how to *come back swinging through your difficult times!*

Section I

WHAT TIME IS IT?

Chapter 1

THE PENDULUM

When I began pulling together my thoughts for this book I found myself reflecting on all the difficult times I have been though. Almost immediately, my attention became focused on the grandfather clock in our church office. It is beautiful, stately, and occupies a prominent space at the end of the hallway.

Often, when I'd have hectic days, packed with one-too-many appointments, I'd race out of my office, glance at the time, and slow my pace because according to the clock, I'd been miraculously graced with a few additional minutes. Then, I would arrive at my meeting, only to find that it had already started. I finally figured out that I had been fooled by the clock's appearance.

At a glance, it certainly looked as if it was functioning properly; however, I realized that instead of looking at the clock's face, I should have been checking its pendulum to see if it was moving from side to side. The secret to the grandfather clock's success resided within the pendulum and its constant movement.

In learning this, I became increasingly fascinated by how grandfather clocks work. The pendulum may look as if it is swinging properly, but if the clock isn't keeping accurate time, something is wrong. Attached to the pendulum is a weight that must be dropped regularly. Failure to do this will ultimately cause the pendulum to stop swinging altogether.

I've learned from my late arrivals that while the clock may have appeared to have it altogether, signs that it didn't, such as being two or three minutes off. This served as a warning and confirmed that inside the clock, everything was *not* okay. Time was slowly but surely coming to a complete halt.

I began thinking of my life's journey as a pendulum swinging me back and forth, often getting stuck on the downside of life. While I certainly enjoyed building a family and building the Inspiring Body of Christ (IBOC) ministry, these episodes of easy living have consistently been chased by episodes of difficult and tragic times.

MY BIGGEST LOSS

When I was 10 years of age, I witnessed something that I never talked about for years. This tragedy stayed locked in my mind, heart, and head like a maimed animal snared in a trap. I knew how important it was to me, but now, as an adult, I understand how valuable it is to others. There are many who are afraid to express that they've experienced tragedy that has caused a life of anger and doubt.

To my neighbors in the low-income neighborhood, even some family members and friends, it was just another 33-year-old who died one day. To me it was a life taken too soon at the hand of reckless teenage boys. In order to fulfill their own greed, lust, and evil desires, they masterminded an attack on the precious gift given by God to raise a future king. And that day I witnessed my mother's violent death.

I came home from school and wasn't feeling well. I knew that my mama would do anything to make me feel better, so I asked for a hamburger from the burger joint up the street. I was upstairs when I heard her return, then I heard the sound of our front door splintering. That's what prompted me to grab the .22 pistol. I looked over the bannister, and when the boys saw me they ran out the back door.

Depression tries to steal our godly perspective.

While lying on the living room floor, my mom comforted me by saying she was all right, but she obviously wasn't. Unfortunately her death was not handled appropriately by the police. As a 10-year-old kid I didn't understand all that my young eyes had seen, and therefore I couldn't reveal the tragic details to them, or anyone else.

In my childish thinking I believed that my selfish desire for a hamburger cost me my mama. And that incessant guilt caused a downward spiral that would change how I viewed life and God for the next 43 years.

Although it was the saddest time of my life, it's what has inspired, motivated, and pushed me into the arena of a survivor of what most people in the public eye are afraid to admit. I was a depressed leader who had to fight through, push through, walk through, crawl through, smile through, and laugh through the pain, confusion, and anger—while still inspiring and encouraging others to not give up. What I lived wasn't just the dark side of life, it was a constant midnight with no signs of daylight on the horizon.

I lived in a constant midnight with no signs of daylight on the horizon.

Sometimes these tragedies plant seeds that don't sprout until years later. To this day I don't like complaining because even if things aren't comfortable, I'd rather just leave it alone than make things uncomfortable for someone else. It has also given me great compassion for the tragedies of others. I've heard a thousand stories of losing a child, war, abortion at age 15, being molested by an uncle, divorce, miscarriage, loss of a business, bad custody decisions, suicide, and people who can't escape inappropriate labels. Because of what I went through, I'm a grateful, gracious, compassionate person.

Discouragement is a traffic jam at the railroad crossing while you wait for the train. The one traffic jam is not the whole journey. If you can wait it out, the arm will rise and you'll cross over. You'll never be without trains in your life; you'll just learn how to graciously wait on them to pass.

I came to realize that God's plan was for me, for all believers, to move through life, enduring both good times *and* bad times. Just like the pendulum, Christians must lose the weight of heaviness and come back swinging their way through difficult times.

Chapter 2

TO EVERYTHING THERE
IS A SEASON

I grew up in a church culture that didn't talk much about depression. In fact, what was emphasized week in and week out was the victory we had in Christ. Even though our victory in Christ was real, there were times when genuine believers, people who loved God, suffered from painful circumstances. If someone became depressed as a result, no one knew about it because no one talked about it—until it was sometimes too late.

Suffering from depression doesn't mean we're suicidal, or have some secret sin in our life, or that God is displeased with us. Experiencing seasons of deflation are absolutely normal even for those of us who love God and have been born again.

I've lived long enough to understand that there is a time for everything under Heaven. That means as people who love

God, we sometimes struggle with seasons of depression, which can look like anything from having a bad day to being in the throes of despair.

Feeling depressed shouldn't be something we're quiet about, but rather something we're completely honest about, bringing it into the light to expose the enemy's attacks. Also, by being honest and forthright, we might help others who are secretly suffering with similar issues.

Our enemy, satan, tries to attack us through depression, and then he tries to isolate us and make us feel too ashamed to talk about it. We assume we're the only ones fighting the blahs and therefore can't be honest about our feelings. *What will people think? What will they say?* When discouragement remains hidden, however, we continue our decline.

What will people think? What will they say?

If someone threw me into a pool, I might be stunned for a moment before swimming back to the edge. But if my arms were bound, I would have no way to even stay afloat. The enemy will attempt to disable us before we are thrown into the deep end of the pool.

As I've studied the Bible and lived through the school of hard knocks, I've come to understand that I'm going to have good and bad days. My life is like a pendulum on a grandfather clock, swinging in both directions. My bad days don't mean I love God any less, nor do they mean that He loves me any less. In fact, my bad days usually have nothing to do with my behavior, they are usually brought on by difficult seasons or situations—many times they are attacks from the enemy. *"Be alert and of sober mind. Your enemy the devil prowls around like a roaring lion looking for someone to devour"* (1 Peter 5:8).

But even though they came from the enemy, they have everything to do with God's plan and purpose for my life. It's crucial to understand that life swings in *both* directions. We will not always have good days, nor will we always have bad days. There is a time for both.

Ecclesiastes 3:1-8 (AKJV) says that there are times and seasons for everything we experience.

> *To every thing there is a season,*
> *and a time to every purpose under the heaven:*
> *a time to be born, and a time to die;*
> *a time to plant, and a time to pluck up that which is planted;*
> *a time to kill, and a time to heal;*
> *a time to break down, and a time to build up;*
> *a time to weep, and a time to laugh;*
> *a time to mourn, and a time to dance;*
> *a time to cast away stones,*
> *and a time to gather stones together;*
> *a time to embrace, and a time to refrain from embracing;*
> *a time to get, and a time to lose;*
> *a time to keep, and a time to cast away;*
> *a time to rend, and a time to sew;*
> *a time to keep silence, and a time to speak;*
> *a time to love, and a time to hate;*
> *a time of war, and a time of peace.*

PAIN IS UNAVOIDABLE

You see, I can't stop pain from happening to me—people will lie about me, my family members will pass away, and I will have to conduct funerals for kids who die before their time. Death is inevitable. Pain is natural.

Even though I can't stop pain from happening to me, I can determine how it will affect me. How long I stay in pain depends on how I respond to it. This isn't true only for me, but for every person who has ever breathed air upon this earth. We have to accept the fact that we will experience painful circumstances.

Not only have I suffered tremendous victories, I've also had times of depression. Sometimes it has lasted for hours, weeks, and sometimes for months. Through each season, my pendulum kept swinging. Though my losses were real and the circumstances were painful, I can honestly say that I've come out on the other side swinging harder than ever before. With every season of depression, there is also a season of joy for which God is preparing us. God causes our lives to swing in perfect balance, giving us opportunities to trust Him all along the way.

WE WILL EMERGE VICTORIOUSLY

Even though we love God and have seasons of suffering, the good news is that we are in good company. In the Bible, the apostle Paul suffered with a thorn in his flesh, a messenger of satan sent to attack him; Job lost all that he had—children, possessions, property, and prestige, yet he still worshiped God; Jesus restored Peter after he denied Him; and Moses pleaded with God to kill him because the children of Israel were so unruly on the way to the Promised Land (see 2 Corinthians 12:7, Job 1:1-22, John 21:15-19, Numbers 11:15). Although each of these men went through a season of downtime, they all came out swinging on the other side, ultimately walking into their God-given destinies.

TWO KINDS OF DEPRESSION

Although I sympathize greatly with anyone who suffers from clinical depression, this book does not address that physiological condition, which is normally treated by a doctor using a combination of therapy and medication. Clinical depression is different. It doesn't just go away!

Whether the depression stems from internal chemical imbalances or it is the end result of some external event that happened to you, the physical symptoms of depression and negative emotions cling to you.... The emotions remain and the problem becomes chronic rather than something that simply passes. Thus a "normal" depression may translate from a simple, natural emotional state of mind to an actual emotional *disorder,* and this is when you need to reach out and get help to get back to as normal a life as possible.[1]

> It's all right to have big problems because you have a big God.

Instead, this book addresses *situational* or *reactive depression,* which is primarily caused by outward circumstances. We all have those seasons when it feels like everything is going wrong and life couldn't get any worse. Each of us experiences these temporary, day-to-day mood changes, which are driven mostly by loss, emotional fatigue, or physical stress. These situations come from time to time; they attack from the outside for a specific period of time until the situation resolves or you work through to a resolution.[2]

THIS TOO WILL PASS

Dear reader, it is my desire throughout this book to help you understand that even if you go through seasons of depression, you are still all right. I want you to know that this season of life won't last forever. It eventually will pass. God is faithful and will not let you be tempted beyond your ability, but He will also provide a way of escape so you can bear it (see 1 Corinthians 10:13). It is my desire that you are equipped to come out of this hard season stronger and more on fire for God than you ever thought possible.

When it looks like I'm drifting and moving back into a period of sadness, I tell my friends to "talk me back!" If you've been stuck on the opposite side of better for way too long, get ready to start moving again. It's time to face your fears, focus your faith, and come out swinging!

NOTE

At the end of most chapters, you'll find some helpful tools, including a chapter summary titled *What I Really Want You to Remember* and a Video Link to view a video that reinforces the main message of the chapter. I also include quotes from what my church members affectionately call "Wisdom from the

Rick-tion-ary"—inspirational quotes taken from a collection of powerful sermons I've taught over the past 44 years.

I know that if you invest a little time to work through this application section you'll exponentially increase the amount of help you receive from this book. So grab a pen. Your healing is calling.

WHAT I REALLY WANT YOU TO REMEMBER

Living in a fallen world guarantees we'll have up and down seasons. This is normal and we shouldn't try to hide them. Situational or reactive depression is the name we give these temporary seasons. Clinical depression is more serious and requires professional help. Times of depression are typical and—like the pendulum—we must swing through to good times and not let ourselves get stuck in the negative. The Bible is full of stories about people who experienced these same seasons that plague us today. God is faithful to provide a way of escape as we walk through these seasons with Him.

APPLICATION EXERCISE

1. What is the difference between situational depression and clinical depression? Which one do you think you are suffering from?

    _____

    _____

2. If the answer is clinical depression, are you willing to get help? From whom will you seek help? Look up the phone number and make that call now. Seriously, call now.

   _____

   _____

3. If you have situational depression jot your thoughts below. Have you ever considered that what you're going through is a season? That it's normal? That you'll eventually come out the other side?

   _____

   _____

4. Encourage yourself throughout the day with this thought: It's a temporary season that the Lord will help me walk through.

SCRIPTURE MEDITATION

God is faithful, and he will not let you be tempted beyond your ability, but with the temptation he will also provide the way of escape, that you may be able to endure it (1 Corinthians 10:13 ESV).

WISDOM FROM THE RICK-TION-ARY

"If God allows you to go through something, then He knows that you are capable of coming out of it victoriously." (3/14/05)

PRAYER

Lord, nothing surprises You. You knew this season was coming in my life and You have already provided a way for me to overcome it. I realize now that my response to this trial is entirely normal. Help me not to be critical of myself but to always look to You as we walk through this challenge together and out the other side into a new season of my life.

VIDEO LINK

www.RICKIERUSH.com/ThePendulum-Ch2

ENDNOTES

1. "Depression Symptoms," What is Depression? http://www.what-is-depression.org/physical-symptoms-of-depression (accessed 8/11/14).

2. Ibid.

Chapter 3

A TIME TO HEAL

During the first few days after my mother's death, I really thought that if I was on my best behavior, I just might be able to reverse this horrific fate and get my mom back. Yet, no matter how hard I prayed, or how diligently I swept our kitchen floor, or dusted every crevice in my room, I soon realized that my mom was never coming back to me. And just when I didn't think life could get any worse, April 20, 1970. It arrived, it was the day we buried Mom.

On the day of her funeral, three things happened that forever changed my life. First, in an effort to comfort me, someone tenderly offered these words from the book of Job, *"The Lord gives and the Lord takes away."* However, instead finding comfort in this Scripture, my 10-year-old mind frantically screamed, *What? God took my mama away? He's the One who killed her?*

And before I could even recover from that first one-two punch, I got knocked down *again.*

While I can't remember his name, I vividly remember one of the ministers was wearing a navy blue, double-breasted suit and a pair of those not-quite-matching blue, fake snakeskin shoes. He had scuffed off the tips of the shoes so that each shoe sort of looked like a snake eye peering out. He stepped up to the mic and said something to the effect of, "God just needed another ROSE for His heavenly garden," and I forgot all about those demonic-looking shoes.

My mother's name was Rose. I remember sitting on that hard, wooden pew thinking, *What? God took my mama away from me because He needed a flower? So, since my mama's name was ROSE, and God needed a rose for His garden, I now get to grow up and go through the rest of my life without my number-one supporter, my cheerleader, my teacher, my mentor, or, as they say in the boxing arena, my cornerman?*

Was this preacher really serious?

Then I distinctly remember thinking, *If God needed flowers, why wouldn't He take Ms. Lily, Little Stevie's mama, or better yet, Mrs. Daisy, the mother of the mean ol' boy who was always trying to take everyone's roll when it was chicken-fried steak day at school? Didn't God need a Daisy in His garden? Besides, everyone always planted roses because the rose was the most popular, most beautiful flower of all, just like my mama.*

I just couldn't figure out what exactly I had done to make God angry enough to pluck my mom away from me, especially at such a young age. Defeated, I thought, *If God could part and hold back an entire sea, so people could walk across on dry land, and if He could take some dirt and make an actual human, surely He must have known to plant enough roses in His garden, right?*

All of a sudden, sitting right at the front of the church, my whole body was consumed by immeasurable rage and anger, which forcefully evicted my initial feelings of sadness and grief. I questioned why God would take her away from me. I remember thinking, *God should have been happy with my mom; she was the one who had dragged me to church every Sunday and Wednesday!*

Confused and driven by my grief-turned-anger-turned-bitterness, I just assumed losing my mom at 10 years old more than filled God's quota of setbacks He had in store for me. I figured that if I could survive losing her, the rest of my life would be trouble-free. Boy was I wrong! It did not take long before I realized that I was just getting started on my journey of being sucker-punched by the trials of life.

I was a sickly kid, and later in life Guillain-Barre Syndrome caused me to be in a paralytic state. I've endured the removal of a tumor in my head, which resulted in vocal paralysis for six weeks. I've had cervical spinal fusion, been in a coma, and I wage an ongoing fight with arthritis. Since my dear mother's death, I've buried my father, stepmother, stepfather, and beloved brother.

> I was just getting started on my journey of being sucker-punched by the trials of life.

It seemed like every time I managed to pick myself up again, something else—a loss, a disappointment, or just sheer physical exhaustion—was right around the corner, waiting to continually trip me up. All this time I couldn't focus on my pain. I had to be the pastor and meet the needs of others.

MY HEALING BEGINS

For years I struggled with anger toward God, and then one day my healing began. I heard the biblical story of Job. He was a faithful, trusting servant of God, and God blessed him with many sons and daughters and great wealth.

> *In the land of Uz there lived a man whose name was Job. This man was blameless and upright; he feared God and shunned evil. He had seven sons and three daughters, and he owned seven thousand sheep, three thousand camels, five hundred yoke of oxen and five hundred donkeys, and had a large number of servants. He was the greatest man among all the people of the East* (Job 1:1-3).

Satan told God that Job only served Him because he was blessed. God gave satan permission to remove Job's possessions. Through one horrendous disaster after another, satan stripped away all that Job held dear, including his children and his property. Job continued to serve the Lord. Satan said that if Job lost his health he would turn against God. God granted satan permission to attack his health but not to kill him. Job struggled to understand his situation. Three of his friends dropped by to comfort him but ended up giving Job bad advice. In the end God rewarded Job's obedience and restored his health. God also doubled his original riches and the number of children he had.

After reading Job's story, I came to some life-changing conclusions:

1. Job had endured a lot more stunning blows and punches than I had, and he not only survived, he also *thrived!* In the end, Job was blessed with more than he'd ever had.

2. No matter what setback he faced, Job never turned against God, which was remarkable since both his wife and his friends told him that he should "curse God and die."

3. *Most importantly,* I learned that Job and I were a lot alike. First of all, both Job and I had suffered tremendous loss. Next, we both seem to be either headed toward, in the middle of, or bouncing back from a setback! Dealing with setbacks seemed to be a natural part of living! Finally, it seemed that both Job and I had been duped, bamboozled, hoodwinked into believe that *God* was the source of our problems, our knockdowns, our setbacks—but that simply was *not true.*

We waste precious time and energy being upset with God.

Instead of confronting our *real* enemy, we both had wasted precious time and energy being upset with God, the one who was actually sustaining us during and bringing us through our setbacks. God was the one setting boundaries so satan couldn't kill Job.

Once I realized that, I was surprised to start seeing Scriptures that I hadn't really noticed before:

> *All generous giving and every perfect gift is from above, coming down from the Father of lights, with whom there is no variation or the slightest hint of change* (James 1:17 NET).

> *"For I know the plans I have for you," declares the LORD, "plans to prosper you and not to harm you, plans to give you hope and a future"* (Jeremiah 29:11).

> *The reason the Son of God appeared was to destroy the devil's work* (1 John 3:8).

> *God anointed Jesus of Nazareth with the Holy Spirit and power, and how he went around doing good and healing all who were under the power of the devil, because God was with him* (Acts 10:38).

So now that I had cleared up that misunderstanding, I only had two questions: *Who* was our real enemy? Who was working so hard against Job and me? I figured that if I started over again with Job's story, I would find the answer, and I was exactly right.

> *God said to Satan, "Have you noticed my friend Job? There's no one quite like him—honest and true to his word, totally devoted to God and hating evil." Satan retorted, "So do you think Job does all that out of the sheer goodness of his heart? Why, no one ever had it so good! You pamper him like a pet, make sure nothing bad ever happens to him or his family or his possessions, bless everything he does—he can't lose! "But*

what do you think would happen if you reached down and took away everything that is his? He'd curse you right to your face, that's what." God replied, "We'll see. Go ahead—do what you want with all that is his. Just don't hurt him." Then Satan left the presence of God (Job 1:8-12 MSG).

This passage of Scripture changed my life forever. It was critical for me. It meant that God wasn't the one who caused the death of Job's family or his other losses, *nor* was God the one who took my mama.

Job falsely accused God of "giving and taking" away his children and his wealth. And that well-meaning, snake-shoe-wearing preacher at my mama's funeral got it all wrong. I learned that God is the giver of all life. God is not the taker of life. Satan is.

I remember thinking, I've been mad at the wrong person. All this time, satan was the enemy who was behind my mama's death and he had been tripping me up and knocking me down. Then I realized how my false accusations must have hurt God. And that satan had thoroughly enjoyed watching and listening to every last bit, all the while knowing that he was the guilty party.

The Bible promises us 70 years of life, *"As for the days of our life, they contain seventy years, or if due to strength, eighty years"* (Psalm 90:10 NASB). John 10:10 (NASB) says, *"The thief comes only to steal and kill and destroy; I came that they may have life, and have it abundantly."* Based on these two Scriptures, we can conclude that a life can be stolen just like fine treasure. I'm not saying that satan steals everyone who dies. Life does have an expiration date. But satan does steal some people's lives early.

When the truth finally dawned on me, I couldn't help but feel regret and, quite honestly, shame after seeing just how I had allowed the devil to dump *his* baggage, filled with anger, grief, sadness, and bitterness, into *my* life.

I had been so distracted by these evil tools that I didn't even realize who I was supposed to be fighting—satan. Now I had a decision to make, and the way I saw it, I had two options:

Option #1

I could wallow in my shame and regret and see this situation as an obstacle; I could let it stop me from moving forward and living for God. Or...

Option #2

I could ask God for forgiveness, send my regret and shame back to satan, their rightful owner, and see this situation as an *opportunity*. I could use it to learn how to better fight the enemy and start training right away!

Once I identified the real enemy, I knew I needed a game plan that guaranteed total victory! So I did what all the great champions do: I set out to learn everything I could about my opponent. I needed to *know* satan. I had to learn about his background, his purpose *and* his plans against me. It was my *time* to "search" and find out everything I could about the Christian's number one enemy—satan! *"A time to search ..."* (Ecclesiastes 3:6).

STEP ONE TO KNOWING YOUR ENEMY

When satan was in Heaven he was called lucifer. God granted him one of the most coveted positions: praise leader over the choir of angelic hosts. The choir's number one responsibility was to continuously glorify and praise God through song. You might say that lucifer was God's "hype man."

When lucifer should have been thanking God for trusting him, he was, instead, becoming more and more envious of God. He couldn't stand the fact that the angelic hosts were praising God and *not* him. He wanted all the glory for himself. Left unchecked, his pride became so all-consuming and expansive that he eventually decided he wanted to be God. And he convinced one-third of the remaining angels to help him in his prideful rebellion.

God swiftly and decidedly delivered a blow to satan that was so powerful that it literally knocked him and his demons right out of Heaven. In Luke 10:18 (NASB) Jesus says, *"I was watching Satan fall from heaven like lightning."* He fell straight down to Earth, splattering and scattering his evilness over the entire, dark, formless, void planet.

NEW AND IMPROVED PRAISERS

Meanwhile, since God needed some new praisers, He decided that He would improve His former model, given the fiasco that occurred with satan. God decided to create a man, who would be the "new and improved" praiser and worshiper.

To accomplish this, the Bible tells us that God said, *"Let us make mankind in our image,"* in reference to God the Father, God the Son, and God the Holy Spirit (Genesis 1:26). Thus, man received a triple blessing, as he was made in the likeness of the Holy Trinity. This "new and improved" man set out to accomplish what satan's pride would not let him do: continuously worship and praise God.

THE ENEMY'S PURPOSE AND PLAN

Knowing that he had absolutely *no* power or authority over God, satan plotted to go after the next best thing—God's children. There's nothing as painful to parents as having something negative happen to their children.

So, satan's main *purpose* was to steal man away from God by killing us or destroying our faith. He knew that if he could use "difficult times" to turn us against God (as he tried to do with me when my mom died), we would never know about the victorious plan He has for our lives. And thanks to Adam and Eve, satan's plan got off on the right foot!

ADAM AND EVE

After God made man, He planted a garden in Eden and filled it with beautiful trees including the Tree of Life and the Tree of Knowledge of Good and Evil. God told Adam, *"You can eat from any tree in the garden, except from the Tree-of-Knowledge-of-Good-and-Evil. Don't eat from it. The moment you eat from that tree, you're dead"* (Genesis 2:16-17 MSG).

Satan, disguised as a serpent, showed up and convinced Eve to rebel against her heavenly Father by eating the forbidden fruit. Unfortunately Adam chose to do the same.

Can you picture a rebuked, yet hopeful satan hissing, slinking, and slithering off to a sideline seat, where he eagerly anticipates his ultimate triumph? Satan just knew that Adam and Eve's rebellion would break their relationship with God—just like his rebellion had broken his relationship.

The "Good" News and the "God" News

You should know that satan has definitely devised a very thorough plan to get us "stuck" in our difficult times. He wants us to stay in a dark, desperate place, whereby we get so depressed and despondent that we just give up on God. However, the "God" news and the "good" news is that He created us in His image, and He has already defeated the enemy on our behalf.

Remember in Genesis 1:26 when God stated, *"Let us make mankind in our image..."*? And then He did exactly what He said. *This is the Good News and the God News!* The results of our spiritual paternity tests are indisputable: *"But you are a chosen people, a royal priesthood, a holy nation, God's special possession..."* (1 Peter 2:9). And because of our birthright, His victory over the enemy is our victory over the enemy! So, come back swinging through difficult times; the victory is already yours! We'll look at how to enforce this victory in coming chapters.

What I Really Want You to Remember

When I was 10 years old, satan deceived me into believing that God took my mother. I was angry and bitter for years as I lived through one trial after the other. Fortunately, from the book of Job, I received a life-changing realization—that God is the Giver of Life and satan is the thief. I also learned that Job survived and thrived in spite of bad counsel and that I was a lot like Job. We'd both been through harrowing losses and we'd both been duped into believing God was responsible. I could continue to wallow in my situation or I could ask for forgiveness and use this opportunity to start fighting satan, the true enemy. Satan is out to hurt God and the way he does that is to attack us—God's children. Satan tricked Adam and Eve into sinning; but amazingly, God didn't disown them like He did satan. In an amazing demonstration of His love for you, God defeated the enemy on your behalf and counted it as your victory.

APPLICATION EXERCISE

1. Prayerfully ask God if there are things you've blamed on Him that were the enemy's responsibility or your poor choices. If so, ask for forgiveness.

   _____

   _____

2. Who is your true enemy?

   _____

   _____

3. If satan was planning a strategy session on how he could make you angry at God or make your life miserable, what would his plan be? Are there specific areas of weakness that he would target?

   _____

   _____

4. How can you stand against him in these areas?

   _____

   _____

SCRIPTURE MEDITATION

I know what I'm doing. I have it all planned out—plans to take care of you, not abandon you, plans to give you the future you hope for (Jeremiah 29:11 MSG).

WISDOM FROM THE RICK-TION-ARY

"The acknowledgment of pain isn't a sign of weakness, it's necessary for our healing." (12/4/02)

PRAYER

Lord, You are the Giver of all life and You are the Giver of all good gifts. I repent for blaming You for the work that the enemy has done. Give me discernment to know the difference between Your voice, the enemy's voice, and my own voice. Help me to send my regret and shame back to satan, their rightful owner, and see my situation as an opportunity to learn how to better fight the enemy.

VIDEO LINK

www.RICKIERUSH.com/ThePendulum-Ch3

Section II

HAVE YOU STOPPED TICKING?

Chapter 4

INTRODUCING...THE *REAL* ENEMY

If we are to be victorious over the enemy's tricks and evil plots, and exercise better judgment and decision making than Adam and Eve did, we need to find the answers to these three critical questions:

1. What does satan look like?

2. How does satan operate?

3. What is satan's house-hunting strategy?

WHAT DOES SATAN LOOK LIKE?

QUESTION: What does satan look like?

ANSWER: Anything that is not of God. He is called the deceiver.

When kids go trick or treating, they disguise themselves. They knock on strangers' doors to "trick" people who don't know them into giving them something. In the same way, satan understands that if he comes as himself you won't give him a chance, but if he comes in disguise he might gain admittance. *"Satan himself masquerades as an angel of light"* (2 Corinthians 11:14). We must be careful who we allow into our lives. Who is he masquerading as? Whoever is behind the mask.

A Force of Nature

Satan also comes as a force of nature. He can get behind the breeze that you use to fly a kite and transform it into a destructive tornado. The same water that you love to swim in, satan blows on it and it becomes a hurricane. Ephesians 2:2 refers to him as *"the prince of power of the air"* (AKJV). The same airways that bring us worship music also bring us horrible music and distracting social media. He will empower any entrance we give him.

Since we are the crown of God's creation, we have free will—the ability to make decisions. Wind and water can't do that. But we have been given the power to recognize him and put him in his place when we see his actions. We have dominion over the earth and over him. We need to detect and evict him by casting him out in Jesus' name: "In the name of Jesus, GET OUT AND STAY OUT!"

Disease

Satan works through nature to do his damage, but he's not limited to that. He can come like an illness—he can look like cancer. He houses himself inside healthy bodies so when he's manifested, he produces death.

Sometimes people will say, "I asked God to take away my cancer." God won't take it away because He didn't give it to you. There is no sickness in Heaven.

Acts 10:38 (ISV) clearly states that disease is an oppression from the devil:

> *God anointed Jesus of Nazareth with the Holy Spirit and with power, and because God was with him, he went around doing good and healing everyone who was oppressed by the Devil.*

Luke 13 records Jesus' healing of a crippled woman. A few verses later Jesus plainly tells us the source of this woman's infirmity.

> *On a Sabbath Jesus was teaching in one of the synagogues, and a woman was there who had been crippled by a spirit for eighteen years. She was bent over and could not straighten up at all. When Jesus saw her, he called her forward and said to her, "Woman, you are set free from your infirmity." Then he put his hands on her, and immediately she straightened up and praised God* (Luke 13:10-13).

A few verses later we see Jesus refer to this infirmity as satan's bondage: *"This dear woman, a daughter of Abraham, has been held in bondage by Satan for eighteen years. Isn't it right that she be released, even on the Sabbath?"* (Luke 13:16 NLT).

If you want to get rid of the problem, send it back to the source. Tell cancer, sickness, depression, disease, and failure to go back to satan where they belong. He is the giver of sickness, disease, and death.

Humans

God is a Spirit, Jesus is a Spirit and the Holy Spirit is obviously a Spirit. God operates through our spirit. The Holy Spirit speaks to us through our spirit. In the same way, satan seeks to operate through our spirit. He likes to work through a body or personality as he seeks to bring destruction.

I am sure you can think of many times when satan has worked through humans. It sounds a lot like this:

- "What can one drink hurt?"

- "Your life will be complete when you finally get a man."

- "Putting in all these extra hours will bring that promotion you're after."

- "We're too smart to get caught."

- "You deserve this."

- "You can quit any time."

- "Wear this dress—he won't be able to take his eyes off you."

- "It'll make you look cool."

Stop for a moment and look at the people who are around you, or just look in a mirror. *So, what does satan look like*? The answer is simple: satan occasionally looks like you and me. We are all potential "houses" where satan can take up residence, so he can execute his devilish plan. He knows how to make himself attractive, and he is always on his best behavior when he is seeking a residence. He's a crafty chameleon but the real scoop about him is found in the following profile.

THE ENEMY'S BACKGROUND CHECK RESULTS
Applicant's Profile Information

APPLICANT'S NAME: (FIRST, MIDDLE, LAST)	Lucifer Beelzebub God-Hater
SOCIAL INSECURITY #:	666
PREVIOUS ADDRESS:	777 Streets of Gold Heaven
REASON FOR MOVE:	Total Eviction
CURRENT ADDRESS:	666 Ubiquitous Ave. Earth, Realm
OTHER KNOWN ADDRESS:	It's Hot In Here Street Hell, Underworld
PROFESSION:	Choir Director/Praise Leader
PREVIOUS COMPANY:	Heavenly Host Choir
PREVIOUS COMPANY'S OWNER:	God our Father
PREVIOUS EMPLOYMENT STATUS:	Terminated and banned from the premises!
REASON FOR SEPARATION FROM PREVIOUS COMPANY:	Tried and found guilty on multiple felony counts: 1. Treason 2. Failed corporate take-over
OTHER CONVICTIONS FOR FELONY OFFENSES:	Stealing, killing, and destroying God's most prized possession: His children
OTHER MISDEMEANOR CONVICTIONS OFFENSES:	Jealousy, envy, pride, hatred, anger, bitterness, grief, sickness spreader, etc.
VERDICT ON ALL CHARGES:	Guilty as charged; sentenced to life in torment
PROFESSIONAL SKILLS/ CHARACTERISTICS:	Lying, cheating, manipulating, imitating, snooping, eavesdropping, hating, strife, unforgiving, etc.

KNOWN TACTICS/ STRATEGIES:	Using unsuspecting humans, including loved ones, friends, and strangers, to carry out his evil plan to keep God's kids separated from our Daddy
OTHER KNOWN ALIASES:	Beelzebub, Satan, Devil, Legion, Liar, Deceiver, The Accuser, Prince of Darkness, the Enemy, etc.
CURRENT WHEREABOUTS:	Roaming to and fro on the earth...seeking to devour
STEPS TO TAKE WHEN (NOT "IF") YOU SEE HIM:	Step 1: Stand boldly (God has not given us the spirit of fear; see 2 Tim. 1:7). *Tip: Don't be afraid of the enemy's loud roar; he's just putting on a front!* Step 2: Cast him (and all his demonic buddies) back to the pits of hell, their permanent home. Step 3: Tap into your power source to ensure the completion of the mission and declare: "In Jesus Name!"

"Satan" means adversary. He is God's enemy and the enemy of all God does and all God loves. He is also called "the devil," which means false accuser. This was the role he played in the book of Job when he attacked Job's character before the Lord. He is also known as the tempter, the wicked one, and the accuser of the brethren (see 1 Thessalonians 3:5, Matthew 13:19, Revelation 12:10).

Now that you know who your enemy is, let's dig deeper.

HOW DOES SATAN OPERATE?

People are spirits living in a human house on this planet. Because satan is a spirit he tries to execute his devilish plan by taking up residence in the body, mind, and/or heart of humans.

Of course as Christians we can't be possessed by the devil, but we can be oppressed by him.

Remember when Peter told Jesus that he shouldn't go to the cross? Jesus replied, *"Get behind me, Satan! You are a hindrance to me. For you are not setting your mind on the things of God, but on the things of man"* (Matthew 16:23 ESV).

Peter wasn't possessed by satan, but he was being influenced by him. Peter was used as satan's mouthpiece. He was using human logic and playing the part of Jesus' adversary. Peter was actually opposing God's divine plan to bring salvation to all people. How's that for doing satan's dirty work?

WHAT IS SATAN'S HOUSE-HUNTING STRATEGY?

Satan uses a very clever, house-hunting strategy. He follows three basic steps:

Step 1: Research the market to identify valuable property.

Step 2: Wait for the right season to buy.

Step 3: Make sure the home fits the buyer's/renter's needs.

First, like any good house-hunter, satan starts his search by seeking information regarding the housing market. He has little interest in cheap, worthless houses, as he can gain access to those at any time. He locates the good neighborhoods with valuable houses and observes the market, patiently waiting to see if the price fluctuates.

He knows that when homeowners are discouraged and struggling through difficult times they tend to focus only on what they can actually see. Then they are more prone to sell at discounted rates. Satan *loves* these "down" seasons, as he can purchase a lot of quality homes with minimal effort.

Once he finds a "good deal" in a valuable neighborhood, he studies the attributes of the house and compares them to his own needs. For example, is the house spacious and empty? Satan just loves that. It means that there is plenty of room to accommodate him, his legions of demonic fiends, *and* all their baggage.

By the way, it does not bother satan if he finds a good deal, but the owners refuse to sell. He will wait patiently, looking for an opportunity to gain entrance, and when we give him that opportunity, he will *always* take it.

What does this mean for you?

1. No matter who you are, or what your background is, you have God's DNA, and therefore, *you are valuable*. Satan is only interested in valuable properties. When you face difficult times, take it as a sign that you are *valuable;* otherwise, satan wouldn't be interested in you.

Your ongoing fight with the devil is a sign that God has given you amazing gifts to share with His people, and satan is desperately trying to find ways to stop you from realizing your potential. Your gift is what continues to make your "property value" rise!

I'm always a little surprised when people wonder why there is so much hell in church and among "church people." I always think, *Why wouldn't there be a lot of hell in the church? The church is the "neighborhood" that contains the most valuable property on earth. Where else would satan take up residence?* You should not be surprised nor deterred by the enemy's ongoing assaults on those who are fervently seeking Christ. Our seasons of difficult times are not accidental; they are *right on time.*

2. Satan is *studying and learning about you.* He is very, very clever and very, very patient. He has all the time in the world to learn your weaknesses. Then he patiently waits for one of your weaknesses to cause you to "dip in your market value."

3. His plan of destruction involves a slow but steady assault that, if not defended properly by going to church regularly and staying in God's Word, will slowly chip away at our foundation. It reminds me of the process used by a demolition crew tearing down a useless building. The demolition crew spends a lot of time making plans. They study the architect's blueprints, identify the structural damage that has already been done, identify points of weakness in the foundation, and carefully formulate a step-by-step plan before they even plant one stick of dynamite.

Like the demolition crew, satan knows that if he takes the time up front to figure out our weaknesses and to plant within us harmful seeds of destruction, our foundation will be so weak that his destruction process will be effortless.

The enemy is a smart, thorough researcher who identifies and exploits our weaknesses, as he plots our ultimate destruction. In order to protect your house—your heart, mind, and body—you must learn to recognize him, his strategies, and the evil, destructive tools he uses. Jesus tells us how to make sure our foundation is secure:

> *He is like a man which built an house, and digged deep,*
> *and laid the foundation on a rock: and when the flood*

arose, the stream beat vehemently upon that house, and could not shake it: for it was founded upon a rock (Luke 6:48 AKJV).

The flood that beat vehemently upon the house is the trials and satan's temptations that come at us. None of these can move a soul built on Christ off His foundation.

Build your foundation on Jesus. Do *not* be moved by the enemy and do *not* let him take up residence with you; however, if you suspect he's already made himself at home in your life, it's time for a *baggage check!*

WHAT I REALLY WANT YOU TO REMEMBER

In order to successfully overcome satan, you must be able to answer the following questions:

1. What does satan look like? Anything that's not of God. He's the great deceiver and he disguises himself. He comes as a force of nature, a disease or through people.

2. How does satan operate? He influences us and uses us as his mouthpiece.

3. What is satan's house-hunting strategy? You are valuable, and satan is studying you to discern the right time and the right strategy to move in.

APPLICATION EXERCISE

1. Do you know that you're valuable? Not just to the enemy, but to God?

   _____

   _____

2. What did you find most interesting from the enemy's background check?

   _____

   _____

3. Can you think of a time when satan used another human to influence you?

   _____

   _____

4. What did he say through this person?

   _____

   _____

5. How can you recognize satan the next time he attacks you through a person, force of nature, or disease?

   _____

   _____

SCRIPTURE MEDITATION

God anointed Jesus of Nazareth with the Holy Spirit and with power, and because God was with him, he went around doing good and healing everyone who was oppressed by the devil (Acts 10:38 ISV).

WISDOM FROM THE RICK-TION-ARY

"God has already equipped us with every tool that is necessary for us to defeat satan." (3/28/11)

PRAYER

Lord, help me to be alert and to discern the enemy in whatever form he comes to attack me. Help me also to resist being used by him to bring harm to others. Jesus, I ask that my house's foundation would always be built on the solid rock—You.

VIDEO LINK

www.RICKIERUSH.com/ThePendulum-Ch4

Chapter 5

IT'S TIME FOR A BAGGAGE CHECK

Hit the road, Jack! And don't you come back no
more, no more, no more, no more.
Hit the road, Jack! And don't
you come back no more![1]

Now that you've learned who the enemy is and what his plan is, it's *time* to reveal how he operates, so you can take a good swing at him and send him *packing!*

Consider the following case study entitled, Jodi's Extended-Stay Houseguest.

JODI'S HOUSEGUEST

Jodi had met her current boyfriend through one of those "friend-of-a-friend-of-a-friend" situations. After their third date, he asked Jodi if he could stay over for a "couple of days" while his apartment was being painted. At first, Jodi was a bit reluctant.

She didn't want to compromise her morals, and she had worked so hard to save up money for her first home; she liked her life the way it was—for the most part.

When she mentioned his request to her girlfriends, they encouraged her to "loosen up a little" so she wouldn't mess up this potential relationship. They reminded her that she was the oldest one in their group and shared how hard it was to live without a man. Jodi wasn't that sure about their "loosen up" advice, but she did agree that life wasn't complete if she didn't have someone to share it with. *Where are all the good marriageable males?* she wondered. So, she decided to loosen up a little. *After all,* she told herself, *it's only for a few days, and it's the Christian thing to do, right?*

Jodi heard a knock and opened her door to find her very attractive guest standing on her doorstep with only one, small overnight bag. Taken aback by his deep, honey-coated voice, she smiled sweetly, said, "Hi," and invited him (and his one, small overnight bag) into her home.

One day, weeks later, Jodi found herself thinking about the second bag that she'd found. She was reaching under her bathroom cabinet to grab her make-up bag and ended up cutting her finger on a razor inside his shaving kit. She guessed that he'd unknowingly shoved her makeup bag aside when he placed his bag there and then neglected to zip it.

In her clumsiness, Jodi managed to slice open a good inch of her finger. Even though she ended up having to get stitches and a tetanus shot (because the blade was rusty and infection set in), when she told the story to her girlfriends, she actually bragged about it and was proud to let them know that he had left another bag in her home.

Then at the next week's "girls' night out," Jodi told her friends about how he'd just recently asked her to move her stuff out of one of the drawers in her armoire to make room for "a few more" of the things he'd had stuffed in the gym bag and backpack that he'd most recently brought. He had suggested that the Christian thing to do would be to "Get rid of this stuff. Christians aren't supposed to be flashy or have an abundance of material things." She donated a lot of her clothes and furnishings that she had worked so hard for to local charities.

Jodi's heart fluttered, her eyes misted with tears.

Jodi's houseguest/soon-to-be-boyfriend/hope-to-be-husband was definitely one of a kind. He took her out on dates, cooked her favorite meals, helped with the laundry, and most impressively, he handled her car's upkeep and maintenance. When he offered to do this, Jodi's heart fluttered, and her eyes misted with tears.

Years and years ago, when Jodi was just a little girl, she thought it was so romantic that her dad used to do all the maintenance on her mom's car. He had even done it for Jodi when she started driving, so Jodi thought for sure that this was some sort of sign from God. Every time he would "fill" her car with $4 or $5 worth of gas, he'd say, "Can't have you stranded somewhere on the side of the road, now can we?"

It didn't take long for Jodi to start daydreaming about silky, white dresses, vanilla cake frosting, and popular wedding songs.

Her best friend had remarked, "Wow! I wish I had your life. This good man just fell out of nowhere. You're so lucky." *Yes, I am,* Jodi thought to herself. *Maybe I will attend church on Sunday to tell God all about my "houseguest" and thank Him for sending him to me.*

She wanted to get his love by any means possible.

Another week passed by so quickly, Jodi forgot all about his apartment and the paint job. Once he told her that he would allow her to tell people on his "approved list" that he was her boyfriend, she focused solely on what she needed to do to make him want to marry her. She took on more and more of the things he initially had done for her in an attempt to make him see how valuable she could be to him. She wanted to get his love by any means possible.

She decided to ask him to split the household bills with her, so she could save enough money to cover the costs of their inevitable wedding and the honeymoon. She casually mentioned the possibility of him moving in permanently since so many of his bags were already there.

When she mentioned these ideas, she was surprised to hear him say that he thought his apartment would be ready in the next few days, and he might be moving really soon. "Besides, it would be crazy to waste money to break my lease." Jodi really wanted him to help her with the bills and move in with her, but she didn't want to anger him, so she dropped the conversation and figured she might try again in a week or two.

A few days later, he brought over more bags and mentioned something about a problem with the painters. When he asked her to clear out even more closet space, Jodi was thrilled and gave the charities another round of her things. She prided herself on her spirit of giving and dreamed about the ways in which God was going to bless her for being such a blessing to others.

Over time, Jodi saw less and less of her friends. She cut down on her volunteer hours at the community center, and she started skipping out of Sunday school. She thought this was a pretty good compromise—because she still went to church. She could keep God happy and she had more free time to spend with her boyfriend, especially because he said his new work schedule was more demanding.

When she complained about not spending enough time together, he suggested that she clear her calendar to make sure she was available for him whenever he had a few minutes to spend with her. It seemed to be the perfect answer to her prayer!

It seemed to be the perfect answer to her prayer!

Thinking her friends would be upset with her for skipping out on their regular social gatherings, Jodi was surprised to hear them encouraging her to stay home, so she would be available to spend time with him. The only problem...he seemed to work more and more, which meant Jodi was alone more and more.

In fact, the weekend her friends were away on their annual girls' getaway trip (the one she'd suggested and planned before her "houseguest" arrived), she found herself feeling really down, sitting alone all weekend while her boyfriend "worked." She called to tell him about her loneliness and to ask him to take her out on a date; but he mentioned the puffy bags and dark circles under her sleep-deprived eyes and told her she needed to get some rest.

He expressed regret that she hadn't slept well the previous night because of the noise and commotion he and his buddies made when they moved in his pool table and bar set. Then they drank and played until the early morning. (She thought of how sweet it was that he apologized.) "Besides," he'd told her, "You don't want to put forth the energy to shower and get dressed. Just rest. I only have a few more bags to move, so they can do the finishing touches in my kitchen."

Jodi realized that his apartment manager must have hired the worst paint company in town, as they'd been painting his apartment for almost six months now.

Jodi slept most of the weekend to try to regain her energy. On a midnight trip to the bathroom she dragged herself out of bed, only to trip over two more bags her boyfriend brought in while she slept. With nothing to break her fall, Jodi crashed to the floor, falling flat on her face. And that is when she tasted the metallic, tell-tale sign of a busted lip—blood.

Carefully weaving her way through the darkness, bumping into suitcase after suitcase, Jodi finally made her way to her bathroom where she flipped on the light. Aghast at what she saw, she stared back at the face in the mirror, hardly recognizing the beaten, bruised, and bloody stranger who stared right back at her.

In that moment of isolation, it hit her. It didn't take six months to paint a 500 square-foot, one bedroom apartment. Everything became clear. It was as if the bathroom light she had just flipped on chased away the darkness, illuminating the crooks and crannies that housed all her houseguest's baggage. That's the moment she realized just how cluttered and junked-up her beautiful home had become.

Jodi realized just how much she had changed and adopted her boyfriend's ways. She stared at the stranger in the mirror and frantically searched for any traces of her old self.

She stared in the mirror, frantically searching for traces of her old self.

Where was the young, hard-working lady who helped out at the community center during her free time? Where was the daughter who had been taught to always keep her house clean and in order? Where was the servant who went to both Sunday school and Sunday morning worship because she knew she needed to have a strong relationship with God in order to always hear His voice?

Did that person still exist inside this bedraggled mess that stared back at her? And if she was still in there, what did Jodi need to do in order to clean things up and get moving in the right direction?

First and foremost, if Jodi is going to "clean" her house, she must first find all the tools and bags and pack them up, so she can send them back to their rightful owner—satan.

ANALYZING SATAN'S BAGGAGE

The following are key points regarding satan's baggage.

It's attractive:

Satan's baggage is attractive. The wrapping is nice, the suitcases aren't scuffed and scratched. The wheels are greased and roll smoothly over your door's threshold. He always uses people who have something attractive to offer you. He comes *"as an angel of light"* (2 Corinthians 11:14). He can and does look like a good friend, a family member, a potential boss with a high-paying job, a potential spouse, etc. Remember, satan will use whoever he thinks has the best chance at getting you to open the door to your heart, mind, and/or body.

There's a lot of it, and it's filled with a lot of his tools:

Satan never reveals the number of bags he actually plans on dropping off at your house, nor does he reveal the evil tools he plans on using to tear you down, get you stuck, and ultimately destroy you. In fact, he drops off the tools in bits and pieces over time so when you finally show weakness, he has all the materials he needs to carry out his plot to separate you from God.

Everything in it and about it is meant for evil:

Every tool, every bag has a destructive meaning and purpose; and regardless how big or small, innocent or harmful you might think a tool is, you need to recognize that satan will use it either alone or in conjunction with other tools for your destruction.

While there are many points of consideration concerning Jodi's case, let's explore a few, select aspects:

OBSERVATION 1:
Satan knows what attracts us and he uses it to gain entrance into our residences without us even realizing it.

In Jodi's case, satan studied her and waited patiently for her to open her door just the slightest bit.

Imagine him sitting at the table next to her and her girlfriends, eavesdropping on their conversation and taking copious notes about what Jodi was attracted to and desired. He knew she was more focused on finding a man than finding time to spend worshiping God. He saw her pained expression when her girlfriends said, "After all, Jodi, you are turning 35 this year." When satan heard her say, "I'm not complete without a man." That's all he needed to hear. Jodi set herself up with her own negative talk. He knew that he would be able to water this seed of negativity later to accomplish his purpose.

Prayers versus Complaints

Many people don't realize that *God only answers prayers*, not complaints. Satan, on the other hand, answers complaints! He hears everything we say, sees everything we do, and can counterfeit what God has created.

Here's how this works:

GOD ONLY ANSWERS PRAYER!	SATAN CAN ONLY ANSWER COMPLAINTS!
"Father, in the name of Jesus, You said that if I will speak whatsoever I desire and seek You first, You would grant me the desires of my heart at the right time...nevertheless, at Your will, Lord...."	*"No matter how hard I try, I just can't seem to find a man who is marriage material, Father. Every time I think I have finally found the one, he turns out to hurt me even worse than the last one. Tell me where to look, God, so I can go and find this man—now."*

Once satan saw this "open-door" opportunity, he knew the best way to approach Jodi. He came in subtly through a trusted friend and a handsome houseguest, showering her with the much-desired affection and care, so he could take advantage of her. He even imitated her dad, who was her childhood hero, thus extending his lease at her house indefinitely.

And when satan tricked her friends into endorsing her idea to isolate herself so she'd be available for her boyfriend, satan thought, *This is going to be an easy kill.* Clueless Jodi was thinking about how nice and understanding her friends were! Meanwhile, her boyfriend was bringing in more bags and moving out more of Jodi's principles, beliefs, habits, etc. Before long, Jodi had given away so much of herself that the enemy had almost complete control of every aspect of her life.

No longer socializing as much with her friends and skipping out on Sunday school, worship services and serving others, Jodi was getting more and more comfortable just staying by herself. People who are in these situations will tell you that they have no idea how they got there nor do they have any recollection of the exact moment things started to go bad. "It just happened slowly, over time," they say. "I didn't start out like this," or "I thought I had it all under control."

Jodi was worried about being single at her age, so satan reached into his baggage and had her girlfriends plant seeds of "lack of self-confidence," "self-doubt," "impatience," and "insecurity." By the time her houseguest arrived, satan only needed him to water the seeds that were already there.

Jodi never saw it coming! She never recognized satan's hand slowly stirring up trouble for her. By the time she realized what was happening, she had lost momentum in her relationship with God, missed opportunities to receive God's blessings, lost ground with her girlfriends, and wrecked the house she had worked and sacrificed to build. It was all part of satan's plan to destroy her.

Satan waters the seeds already there.

Whether you are fighting a drug addiction that started with smoking cigarettes as a teen, an abusive situation that initially was just a little anger, a jail sentence that started as a few unpaid speeding tickets, or other seemingly small, regrettable lapses in judgment, you must recognize these issues have grown out of tools and seeds that satan had hidden in his baggage.

Conduct a thorough baggage check—find satan's tools, pack them up, and send them back to him.

We must remember that satan isn't trying to harm or injure us; he is actually trying to kill us with every and all attacks he launches; he will and does use any attraction to lure us away from God's plan and purpose for our lives.

OBSERVATION 2:
Use hindsight to enhance your 20-20 vision the next time satan rings your doorbell. You may get tripped up again, but you may be able to break your fall and recover more quickly!

First, Jodi realized in hindsight that if she'd spent as much time learning about her houseguest as he'd spent learning about her, she may have been able to grab something to break her fall. She might have saved herself some bruises and a busted lip. There were little signs all along the way that she missed because her vision was blurred by the misconception that she needed a man to be fulfilled.

It is too bad that the same Sunday her pastor preached on the "Dangers of Being Blinded by Blurred Vision," her boyfriend told her, "I'll be back at ten and take you on a romantic picnic in the park." After all, she'd been complaining about not getting to spend much time with him. She was so excited and felt really special when he said he was taking some time off work for her! Although she hated the fact that he set the time for Sunday, right when she should be at morning worship service, she skipped church anyway.

Looking back at the date, she remembered that he ended up staying later at work. In hindsight, she realized that she could have attended both Sunday school and worship service and still made it home in time for her date. Consequently, she missed the "special delivery" message that God was sending specifically to her!

Additionally, if Jodi would have stopped and turned on the light in her bathroom the day she was looking for her makeup bag, she might have found her boyfriend's shaving kit and seen the sharp, rusty razor that caused her so much pain and suffering, not to mention the costs for her medical treatments. After all, she opened that cabinet every day; she could not help wonder how she'd managed to miss finding it when he first moved it in.

In her focus on making him love her, she supposed she got so used to adjusting her routine, principles, and beliefs that she didn't even realize she had started reaching around his stuff to get to hers.

> She missed the "special delivery" message God sent specifically to her!

It's amazing to think that such small items or changes can wreak such large amounts of havoc. This is why it is imperative to continually conduct baggage checks to see what tools satan has slipped in and dropped off in our hearts, minds, and attitudes.

What tools of heaviness or weight has satan dropped around your neck that is slowly but surely wearing you down and bringing you to a complete stop?

OBSERVATION 3:
Satan hides baggage of all shapes and sizes throughout our hearts, minds, and bodies so that he can attack us when the right season comes. He is constantly tripping us up and knocking us down, even when we think we know where we are, he still manages to make us fall.

What's more, satan used Jodi's boyfriend to show up during the right season. He caught her at the beginning of one of her "down seasons" when Jodi was already frustrated because she didn't have a boyfriend. Right from the start, satan used Jodi's girlfriends to influence her to go against her own principles and better judgment. Jodi had no idea about all the evil tools satan had crammed into that small, overnight bag: jealousy, strife, anger, depression, hatred, unforgiveness, etc. All these are the hidden tools the enemy uses to attack us.

Since Jodi treated him nicely, he took that to mean that she would tolerate living with him and all his baggage. He could continue to take up more and more space, increasing the size and weight of his destructive baggage. Little by little he moved in more of his evil tools as Jodi spent less time in prayer, got less and less sleep, became less concerned about her personal appearance, lost interest in her friends and hobbies, and became more and more moody. Satan gradually wore her down so much that she barely recognized herself. This is the enemy's plan.

Satan is a crafty, subtle house-hunter, who only goes after the most valuable property. If that happens to be your house, you may want to perform a background check, so you recognize him from the outset. He is not interested in doing any home improvement;

he only works to tear down. This being the case, if you want to survive, you must continuously conduct your own thorough baggage checks to find the enemy's hidden, fatal-intended tools. Then you can declare to him, "Hit the road, Jack, and don't you come back no more!"

REMINDERS

1. Everyone has baggage.

Like Jodi, we all have our own baggage case studies from various seasons in our lives that need examining. We all find ourselves tripping over the baggage satan has been hiding in our hearts, attitudes, and bodies since we were children.

In my case, the anger that I felt toward God after my mom died was a tool that the enemy continually used to keep me from reaching my God-given potential. Whether my anger kept me from getting a good job or caused me to lose very close friends, this baggage was heavy, and its weight kept me from achieving my purpose.

Feeling like you are getting knocked down or held back at every turn, or never accomplishing your goals or reaching your full potential can be overwhelming and cause you to give up. I have learned that people seem to have an easier time navigating these seasons once they accept the fact that they are always in one of these three seasons of life:

- coming out of difficult times, or

- headed into difficult times, or

- standing right in the middle of difficult times.

Much like the pendulum in a grandfather clock, we find ourselves swinging in and out of these "due seasons" in our own "due time," just as declared in the book of Ecclesiastes.

In Jodi's case, she was swinging right into a difficult time, unaware that satan had already been using others to drop off his bags of evil tools to ensure he tripped her up and she fell. While he is delighted with her falls, you must remember that his ultimate goal is to make sure her fall is so hard and so damaging that she gives up on God and elects to stay down and remain stuck in her difficult situation. *This* is exactly what the enemy wants and exactly what he sets out to do to all God's children. That means you really need to know all you can about the enemy.

2. Learn everything you can about your enemy so you can recognize his baggage and send him packing!

I also want to remind you not to focus on the wrong enemy. While Jodi should dump her boyfriend because he's not a Christian, it's not the boyfriend who is her main enemy. It's the spirit that's influencing him. Don't fight the people in your life, fight the spirits influencing them.

> *For we are not fighting against flesh-and-blood enemies, but against evil rulers and authorities of the unseen world, against mighty powers in this dark world, and against evil spirits in the heavenly places* (Ephesians 6:12 NLT).

Take time to learn everything you can about your enemy satan and his baggage. Consider seriously the following questions:

- What does satan look like?

- What is satan's purpose and plan?

- How does he operate?

- What strategies does he employ to carry out his mission?

- What tools does satan use?

- Who helps him carry out his purpose?

- How do I maintain complete victory over satan?

We must seek the answers to these questions, and then use that knowledge to prepare our hearts, minds, and bodies for battle. Failure to do so ensures that our doorbells will constantly ring, and we'll find ourselves facing unwanted, uninvited, and unwelcomed extended-stay houseguests on a regular basis. Arm yourself with knowledge from God's Word. Shore up support from your worship and fellowship experiences. Otherwise, you will be unarmed, unprepared, and unable to defeat satan, guaranteeing your ultimate *death*.

So, now let's get the eviction notice ready!

WHAT I REALLY WANT YOU TO REMEMBER

Jodi's case serves as a metaphor for how satan operates. He slowly but surely takes up residence in our lives as an uninvited, unwanted, and unwilling-to-leave extended-stay houseguest.

Through Jodi's story, you can identify the evil tools satan hid in the baggage he continually dropped into her life. These are the tools he uses to kill, steal, and destroy God's children; you need to know how to identify them so you can pack them up, address them to satan at 666 Hell and Damnation Drive, Purgatory, and ship the enemy the tools he left behind. It's time to do some *baggage checks!*

APPLICATION EXERCISE

1. Do-it-yourself baggage check! Identify the tools satan has hidden in your heart, attitude, and/or body:

   ▪ Are you more sensitive?

   _____

   _____

   ▪ Has your attitude become more ungodly?

   _____

   _____

   ▪ Do you find yourself holding on to anger that is so powerful it seems to fill your entire being?

   _____

   _____

   ▪ Instead of praising God for your comeback, do you find yourself complaining more?

   _____

   _____

   ▪ Are your so-called "blessings" costly? Is your supposed "marriage-material" boyfriend making your life better or worse? Are you losing more than you're gaining?

   _____

   _____

- When you list five words to describe your life, do they reflect undying faith in God to deliver you out of your difficult times?

  _____

  _____

- Are negatives so overwhelming that they dampen your desire or prevent you from getting to church and spending time with God?

  _____

  _____

- Are you housing unforgiveness in the corner behind an acceptance of an apology?

  _____

  _____

- Are you hateful, mean-spirited, and impatient when dealing with others who aren't like you?

  _____

  _____

- What don't you like about your body?

  _____

  _____

- Do you realize that you always have enough energy to go to work or to go out with your friends, but you always seem to get debilitating headaches when it's time to go to worship and spend quality time with God, your Father?

  _____

  _____

2. How is the enemy keeping you stuck so you can't get to the blessings God has already given you?

  _____

  _____

3. Circle anything you're struggling with:

Jealousy	Unforgiveness	Bitterness
Sickness	Shame	Pride
Depression	Isolation	Discouragement
Envy	Unbelief	Distractions
Strife	Conflict	Intimidation
Grief	Deception/Mistrust	Conflict
Hatred	Anger	Accusations

SCRIPTURE MEDITATION

For our struggle is not against flesh and blood, but against the rulers, against the authorities, against the powers of this dark world and against the spiritual forces of evil in the heavenly realms (Ephesians 6:12).

WISDOM FROM THE RICK-TION-ARY

"We must exercise our authority over satan the moment we recognize him." (4/9/06)

PRAYER

Lord, I repent of opening the door to satan. Please help me identify and remove all of his baggage from my life. And next time, help me to have wisdom to sense the enemy's plans before he even moves one tiny bag into my house. Lord, help me to pursue You with as much intensity as the enemy pursues me.

VIDEO LINK

www.RICKIERUSH.com/ThePendulum-Ch5

ENDNOTE

1. Percy Mayfield, "Hit the Road, Jack," (Tangerine Music Corp, 1961), http://metrolyrics.com/hit-the-road-jack-lyrics-ray-charles .html.

Chapter 6

It's Eviction Time!

FROM: Saints of God
TO: The Enemy

EVICTION NOTICE

Please be advised that your place of residence is being over taken by the people of God. So pack your bags. Its time for you to go! We've come to take back everything you've stolen from us! We've come to take back our families, homes, money, cars, churches, children, and our minds! We're ready for war & are armed and dangerous.

"The kingdom of heaven suffereth violence and the violent take it by force." Matthew 11:12

SATAN'S TOTAL EVICTION

Knowing how to evict satan from your life involves using your God-given authority to tell him, "IN THE NAME OF JESUS, GET OUT AND STAY OUT!" Although this may not seem complicated, by now you probably realize that the enemy is far too cunning and evil to make things that easy. He is not going to go away without a fight, so consider everything you've learned about him, check your house to see how he has already used his tools to cause damage. Then consult the utmost Authority and enlist His services to guide and direct you through this process.

Don't allow yourself to be deceived by the apparent simplicity of the eviction process, for you know the enemy is a formidable opponent.

Before we go over the steps to get satan out of your life, you must first understand that we are called to complete a *total eviction. Total* evictions are slightly different from the typical eviction. Total eviction means that we are putting the enemy and all of his baggage *completely out* of our lives. Regardless what the enemy has stolen from us, we must never keep any of his baggage. Instead we rely on God to give back whatever the enemy has stolen from us, just as he did with Job (see Job 42:10-17).

Next, in a total eviction, we must be determined to move swiftly and decidedly in totally evicting satan from our lives.

Finally, we have spent quite a bit of time learning exactly who the enemy can be and how he operates once he finds an "open house." In a total eviction, we apply this knowledge to carefully screen each new applicant. Plenty of time and consideration is given to this process, as we definitely do not want a repeat encounter with satan.

THE EVICTION PROCESS— PUTTING OUT THE ENEMY

Many evictions involve four basic Principles of Total Eviction. Let's consider these in more detail.

1. Total eviction is a formal process and requires that all related details are understood and attended to.

In a literal eviction, homeowners are advised to make sure they have all the necessary documentation in place and knowledge of the process before they start.

In a spiritual eviction, you must arm yourself with knowledge as well. After all, you didn't ask satan to move in, he just showed up. Instead of making a grand entrance, he subtly inserted his influences to affect your heart, mind, and attitude.

Remember, Ephesians 6:12 declares, *"For our struggle is not against flesh and blood, but against the rulers, against the authorities, against the powers of this dark world and against the spiritual forces of evil in the heavenly realms."*

Satan is prepared to use any tool at his disposal, as he is always working fast and furiously to steal from you, to kill you, and to destroy you completely (see John 10:10).

He loves to take bad seeds that he planted when you were a child and watch them bloom into ugly plants of hate. Once you can identify and name his tools, you can start to manage them.

2. Total eviction means getting the tenant out of your house and finding and cleaning out all his baggage.

In a total eviction, you search to confirm that satan has left baggage in your life. Find it, identify it, and pack it up, so it can be sent with him when you kick him out.

As you have learned in previous chapters, it is imperative to conduct your own baggage check. Inspect every closet, scan under every bed, and scour every cabinet to make sure he has not hidden any of his baggage in your house!

Remember, satan's baggage contains toxic, destructive tools he uses to destroy our lives! So whether it's jealously, envy, sickness, depression, strife, anger, grief, hatred, unforgiveness, shame, accusations, conflict, bitterness, pride, or deception, all these evil tools must be packed up and sent right back out of your house along with satan when he goes.

3. Total eviction requires God's assistance.

Without God, what you think you are strong enough to master will actually master you: *"If you think you are standing strong, be careful not to fall"* (1 Corinthians 10:12 NLT).

Ask God for strategies to guide your every move. To try and do it on your own is futile. Luke 24:49 refers to the Spirit of God as *"power from on high,"* which is available to all believers to strengthen them to resist temptations and to effectively abolish the works of satan in their lives.

4. Total eviction is a personalized, hands-on, face-to-face process, which requires mastery over fear and intimidation.

You will need to stand boldly and confront the enemy head-on. But, it is only by God's power and authority granted through His Son and the Sprit that we are able to stand and confront the devil with boldness.

Here are some Scriptures to build your faith:

> *For God has not given us a spirit of fear and timidity, but of power, love, and self-discipline* (2 Timothy 1:7 NLT).

Say to those with fearful hearts, "Be strong, do not fear;
your God will come, he will come with vengeance; with
divine retribution he will come to save you (Isaiah 35:4).

So do not fear, for I am with you; do not be dismayed,
for I am your God. I will strengthen you and help you;
I will uphold you with my righteous right hand (Isaiah
41:10).

Thus says the LORD...I have called you by name, you
are mine (Isaiah 43:1 ESV).

FORCEFULLY AND RESOLUTELY EVICT SATAN

In the case involving Jodi, she made some critical errors. For
one, when Jodi became so frustrated with her boyfriend that she
actually wanted to talk to him, she never directly addressed what
she wanted. And then when she did speak "around" the topic,
she did it all wrong. Instead of speaking directly to the source of
her problems, she instead chose to speak to her boyfriend. This
is most unfortunate, as satan had invaded her boyfriend and was
using him as part of his grand scheme to kill her.

So what should Jodi have done to ensure total eviction?

When you want God to do something, or when you need something, be very clear, very direct, and very specific. While you may
find that it is easier to "think" a conversation with Christ, if you
want to be heard by the enemy, you must verbalize exactly what
you want him to do and what you expect God to do during this
process. The enemy doesn't have the ability to read your mind.

In my book *May I Have Your Order, Please?*, I use an analogy that involves ordering dinner at a drive-thru. While you are looking at the menu options salivating, you can *think* your order all you want *(hamburger, large fries, chocolate shake, make that two chocolate shakes)* but the attendant will not place your order until you actually *say* what you want.

In God's Word, we are taught that we must employ the same strategy when using Christ's power or authority. Mark 11:23 declares, "You shall have what you say."

Say what you want and mean exactly what you say.

Tell satan out loud and with confidence exactly what it is that you want him to do. Say what you want and mean exactly what you say. Speak to him with the power and authority God has granted to you to use in His name. This is one of the many perks of being a believer. You always have access to God's power and authority when you confront the enemy.

I suggest that you memorize the following paragraph. It's a tool to bring you out of bondage. You may need to say it multiple times a day for many days. That's okay. Don't give up.

Satan, I cast you and all of your demons and all your symptoms out. IN THE NAME OF JESUS, GET OUT AND STAY OUT! You cannot have my mind, my spirit, or my body. Today you are totally evicted. God gave me power and authority to cast you out and it's time for you to hit the road. Don't come back. I am victorious. My mind has been restored. My soul has been restored, and I am renewed by the blood of Jesus. In the name of Jesus, AMEN.

Even after you clean your house and strengthen your relationship with God, the enemy is already lurking around, trying to find more cracks to squeeze back through! It's natural—expect it. So, find the cracks in your life that allowed him access to your house in the first place. Ask God to reveal what is missing, and close it off by filling yourself with God's Word and by building a stronger, better relationship with Him. This act represents the Law of Substitution.

THE LAW OF SUBSTITUTION

This law says that when something is removed, it has to be replaced. We learn from Scripture that when satan is cast out of our hearts, we must fill the void with the Word of God and post a "NO VACANCY" sign. The Word of God talks about the dangers of an empty house.

> *Then the spirit finds seven other spirits more evil than itself, and they all enter the person and live there. And so that person is worse off than before* (Luke 11:26 NLT).

In these houses, if we don't get full dosages of the Word on a consistent basis, those empty places serve to attract more demons.

That is why you must instantly post a "NO VACANCY" sign to complete the total eviction process. Once this is done, the enemy has no choice; he must go.

WHAT I REALLY WANT YOU TO REMEMBER

We must be determined to move swiftly and decidedly in totally evicting satan from our lives. We must find, identify, and pack satan's bags so they can be sent with him when he gets kicked out. Ask God to guide your every move. You will have to tell the enemy exactly what it is that you want him to do, "IN THE NAME OF JESUS, GET OUT AND STAY OUT!" Finally, find the cracks in your life that allowed satan access to your house in the first place and fill those abandoned spaces with God's Word. Post a "NO VACANCY" sign.

QUESTIONS

1. Are you willing to evict satan and *all* his luggage?

   _____

   _____

2. Are you asking for God's leading?

   _____

   _____

3. Are you declaring, "IN THE NAME OF JESUS, GET OUT AND STAY OUT!"

   _____

   _____

4. In what areas have you have allowed satan access?

_____

_____

5. Will you write a plan to get rid of satan and then put it into action?

_____

_____

SCRIPTURE MEDITATION

And having disarmed the powers and authorities, he made a public spectacle of them, triumphing over them by the cross (Colossians 2:15).

WISDOM FROM THE RICK-TION-ARY

"If anything in your life doesn't line up with God's Word, kick it out." (10/13/04)

VIDEO LINK

www.RICKIERUSH.com/ThePendulum-Ch6

PRAYER

Lord, I know that I must not allow satan to leave even one tiny piece of baggage at my home. Help me to be willing to surrender every sin, hindrance, and distraction to You. I am trusting in Your grace and strength to help me stand strong against him when he tries to reenter my house.

Section III

You're Right on Time

Chapter 7

IS YOUR PENDULUM STUCK?

I've heard it said that life is 10 percent what happens and 90 percent how we respond.

If there was ever an example of why you should never give up, Dr. Seuss is it. His most famous book, *The Cat in the Hat*, has spread into television and cinema. But all of it nearly never happened. The first book that he completely created himself was rejected by publishers 27 times.

Dr. Seuss was heading back to his apartment to burn it when he bumped into an old college friend who had just started working that very morning as a children's book editor. A few hours later he had signed a contract to publish *And to Think that I Saw It on Mulberry Street*, after it had been rejected 27 times.

That book was never as popular as his later works, but it launched his career. Dr. Seuss was later quoted as saying "If I had been going down the other side of Madison Avenue, I'd be in the dry-cleaning business today."

After he was rejected 27 times he must have felt like his pendulum would never start moving, but he was still sending out his manuscript! Way to never quit swinging!

LIFE EVENTS

You might be thinking, *I'm a Spirit-filled, born-again Christian. How did I end up in the dumps?* Like I mentioned in a previous chapter, satan doesn't move in all at once. He's subtle. Things like loss, disappointment, and exhaustion are tools he uses to discourage you.

Life events just happen and they're not your fault, they're not anyone's fault. We live in a broken, sinful world and bad things happen to good people. The enemy's favorite job is trying to hurt God through messing with His children. That's why he's after us with such a vengeance.

LIFESTYLE CHOICES

Then there are other times when losses, disappointments, and exhaustion occur in our lives because we contributed to or even caused them. These are called *lifestyle choices*. These are the choices you make on your own when you block out God's instructions.

Aristotle is often attributed with saying that humans are *rational animals*. As someone who has pastored for 24 years, I can promise you that while we humans have the ability to be rational, there is no guarantee that we use it. All you need to do to confirm this is read or listen to the news. (Although I highly recommend replacing a steady diet of depressive incidents with something edifying like Christian music, TV programs, or books.)

Sometimes we make poor lifestyle choices because we honestly don't have the information we need. If this happens, wait. Don't decide until you can make a fully informed decision. Here's why—every decision we make comes with consequences. Sometimes they are unpredictable, but many times we know exactly what they are before we choose.

Jonah is a great example of someone who experienced negative consequences when he purposely disobeyed God. He literally ran from his God-given assignment. He tried to escape God's presence and ended up trapped in the belly of a fish. Talk about being in a tough season!

Every decision comes with consequences.

> *In trouble, deep trouble, I prayed to God. He answered me. From the belly of the grave I cried, "Help!" You heard my cry* (Jonah 2:2 MSG).

Jonah continues in chapter 2, verse 7 (MSG):

> *When my life was slipping away, I remembered God, and my prayer got through to you, made it all the way to your Holy Temple.*

Now you won't be swallowed up by a large fish, but God will put roadblocks in your life to show you that you are entering into dangerous territory where satan is waiting for you. This is not to discourage you but to get you back on track with Him.

Galatians 6:7-8 (NASB) says:

> *Do not be deceived, God is not mocked; for whatever a man sows, this he will also reap. For the one who sows to his own flesh will from the flesh reap corruption, but the one who sows to the Spirit will from the Spirit reap eternal life.*

The difference here is pretty clear—reaping corruption or reaping eternal life.

YOUR SIN WILL FIND YOU OUT

When I was about 6 years of age I wanted some candy so badly, but my mom said no. Nevertheless, I knew that she usually had candy in her purse; and when I looked inside, she had a Hershey bar next to another box of chocolate. I grabbed the box and went outside thinking what a wonderful opportunity this was to satisfy my sugar cravings (even though the conditions weren't exactly ethical).

You know how chocolate can sometimes cause an adolescent's face to break out? Well, when this "chocolate" got into my system, it didn't break out on my face, but it did break out. This chocolate was ex-lax!

My mom allowed me to go outside and play knowing all the time that what goes in eventually comes out. After laughing and playing with my friends, I felt a unique sensation building in my gut—it was a tremendous urge, a drive, which propelled me on a mission to go back in the house.

Unfortunately the door was locked. I kicked and knocked and pleaded. "Please, mama, let me in!" She looked at me with a knowing smile and asked, "Ricky did you go in my purse and take some chocolate?" And I said, very convincingly, "No, Mama. I would never steal from you." And as I pleaded to come inside, evidence to the contrary was weighing heavily on my stomach.

I will spare the details for my more sensitive readers, but needless to say she made me face the consequences. She didn't open the door until it was too late. The chocolate seemed good when I thought I had gotten away with it, but it was bad when I realized it hadn't gotten away with me.

And that's how deceptive satan is, he can disguise himself as something you desire just to get into your life so that later he can destroy you from the inside out. (I am happy to say that I am a rehabilitated man. To this day, almost 50 years later, I am ex-lax free!)

Life events and *lifestyle choices* are two ways we can become discouraged. Other life issues that can cause you to become deflated include:

- Chronic health problems

- Loneliness

- Lack of support

- A childhood trauma

- Drug use

- Alcoholism

- Confusion with sexual orientation

Get before the Lord and ask yourself and Him, "Is this difficult season something that just happened or is this something to which I contributed?" If you contributed in any way, I've got great news for you. Just like the father was waiting for his prodigal son, your heavenly Father is waiting and longing for your return.

> *He has removed our sins as far from us as the east is from the west. The Lord is like a father to his children, tender and compassionate to those who fear him. For he knows how weak we are; he remembers we are only dust* (Psalm 103:12-14 NLT).

God has forgiven you, now forgive yourself. Ask the Lord to help you connect at a heart level with these two words from this Scripture: tender and compassionate. The next time you come up short, remember that these two words are how the Father feels toward you.

THREE MORE ENEMY STRATEGIES

Let's look in more detail at three additional strategies the enemy uses to bring us down: loss, discouragement, and exhaustion.

1. Loss

Webster's Dictionary defines loss as "the experience of having something taken from you or destroyed."

After living through the loss of my mother at age 10 and counseling more church members than I can remember, I've come to the conclusion that loss is often the most difficult cause to deal with.

Although all loss can be stressful, I'm going to encourage you to use some perspective to evaluate the intensity of yours. Some losses can be totally disabling and some are merely an annoyance. Sometimes we can take those smaller losses and make mountains out of our molehills. We can waste hours, days, or years fretting over what in reality isn't that big a deal.

When we really put things in focus, much of what we go through on a daily basis is inconsequential. On the news this morning I saw the following events: The Ebola virus is killing people in West Africa. The Middle Eastern conflict is killing Jews and Arabs. There was a mudslide in California and a killer earthquake in China. A storm reached hurricane force, and a ferry capsized in Bangladesh. Those people have something worthy of complaining about. Many times, we don't.

Evaluate the intensity of your loss.

Wants and Needs

Let's examine the difference between a want and a legitimate need. To do this, we need some proper perspective. The dictionary defines perspective as an "accurate point of view or the ability to see it."

The following are some quotes for your enjoyment from those with a "unique perspective" on life and various topics:

> If you're being run out of town, get in front of the crowd and make it look like a parade. —AUTHOR UNKNOWN

If the only tool you have is a hammer, you tend to see every problem as a nail. —ABRAHAM MASLOW

There is no burnt rice to a hungry person. —PHILIPPINE PROVERB

I can't say as ever I was lost, but I was bewildered once for three days. —DANIEL BOONE[1]

And finally, my favorite is from Matthew Henry, author of the well-known Bible commentary.

> **Depression tries to steal our godly perspective.**

Henry always tried to give thanks in all things. One day he was robbed. Here's his perspective about it:

I thank Thee first because I was never robbed before; second, because although they took my purse they did not take my life; third, because although they took my all, it was not much; and fourth because it was I who was robbed, and not I who robbed. —MATTHEW HENRY[2]

Hopefully you enjoyed other people's perspectives, but let's get back to yours.

We all have wants and we all have needs. What is a want from my perspective could be viewed as a need for someone else.

Take the loss of a personal item such as glasses, wallet, keys, or, Heaven forbid, your cell phone. It only takes the loss of your phone to trigger intense emotions. How do you feel? Frustrated? Panicky? Even lost? Your emotions can be all over the place.

One way the enemy gains access is through our feelings. I *feel* like my whole life is contained on my cell. But that's a feeling not a reality. If the enemy can get us worked up over a feeling, he can knock us off balance.

When my phone was lost I had to put it in perspective. After the initial reaction, I realized it was only a *cell* phone and I wouldn't *sell* my peace to the devil over a *cell* phone. Or it's the key to my house, not the key to my future, that I can't seem to locate—perspective.

A negative feeling, worry, anxiety, and stress over minor losses are indicators that we aren't trusting in God as our Protector, our Provider, our Healer, and our Good Shepherd who leads us.

Loss Can Be Traumatic

A loss that may totally deflate one person might have no affect on another. Don't pass judgment on what is a "legitimate" loss in others. That is totally in the eye of the beholder. Losing a tooth in the second grade can be distressing. Kids can be cruel or they can just give the "loser" a hard time because they think it's funny. But, that negative attention may cause the young child to feel as if he or she is not like the other kids or not liked by the other kids. Or the child might become deflated not understanding that another tooth is coming in to replace it.

As a maturing adult, losing your hair can be stressful, especially for men who are looking in the mirror each day and watching their hairline recede like floodwaters on a sunny day. When I was a younger man, my Afro hair style was so big that no one would dare sit behind me in a movie theatre. When I started losing my hair, I knew it was *not* coming back. It was "hair today and gone tomorrow." Every morning I'd look at my hairbrush and wonder, *They were hanging on yesterday, what made them decide to let go today?* I can joke about it now, but it was a real loss that I had to work through.

Anything that affects our appearance can cause us to suffer from low self-esteem, ultimately resulting in limited social interaction. What may seem benign to someone can actually be quite traumatic to the person experiencing it. Put another way, "Puppy love is real to the puppy."

The Greatest Loss

The most damaging loss that people experience is the loss of life. Losing someone you know or love is hard to deal with. Period. Because death is final, this loss is often the one thing that will send you into deep depression. When it is abrupt or sudden, then it is really challenging to see anything positive.

You may blame yourself, the individual (if they committed suicide), or others; and if you don't get closure, this loss can eat away at you for the rest of your life. Satan uses death to deflate us—but death is not God's idea. Nor do we have to stay stuck there forever. This is not to say you will get over the loss, but you *can* get past it.

God's Promises for You

The Church is filled with believers who have experienced loss. It can make you feel as if you are spiraling out of control and that God has abandoned you. But He hasn't. Even in dealing with death, God has a promise for you. He reassures you that He did not take your loved ones; rather, He does have them with Him if they ever accepted Him. God doesn't need another rose in His garden like I was told. He didn't kill your child, spouse, friend, etc. He did not, but He has them there in Paradise. When their body retired, their spirit returned to Him.

The enemy will use tragedy to whisper lies in your ear because his goal is no longer about the person who died, it's now his goal to destroy your faith. Remember in the first section it was clearly stated that satan wants to steal your faith? Taking someone you love is one of his tools. Unfortunately he knows that many Christians have been taught that God takes their loved ones away. So be comforted in knowing that God has your loved one with Him.

When we don't understand the pain we are going through, we sometimes blame God for things He never did. But when we rightly understand who God is in His nature, then we can rest assured that He has a good and purposeful plan for each of us. And even though the enemy will try to steal from us, kill us, and destroy us, Jesus says, *"I am the way and the truth and the life"* (John 14:6). The devil is all about death and destruction. Jesus is all about abundant life.

> **The enemy will use tragedy to whisper lies in your ear.**

Let's visit Job again. His losses were tremendous. He lost all of his children, his livelihood and his health. Then his "friends" who came to comfort him gave him bad advice. It's almost unbelievable to imagine losing that much and still having confidence that God's plan is flawless.

Job said something that many Christians say in order to justify their losses. He uttered these words, *"The Lord gave and the Lord has taken away..."* (Job 1:21). That cannot be further from the truth when it comes to God's plan for our lives. God only seeks to add to you; taking away from you would leave you in a state of distrust and discouragement.

As I learned earlier from the book of Job, satan is the thief. God is the Giver of life. All goodness comes from His hand. He gave Adam and Eve life in a garden paradise; and through deception, satan took it.

The devil is all about death and destruction. Jesus is all about abundant life.

Let's examine what the Scriptures say about this: *"Every generous act of giving and every perfect gift is from above and comes down from the Father who made the heavenly lights, in whom there is no inconsistency or shifting shadow"* (James 1:17 ISV).

The author of Hebrews states, *"...because anyone who comes to him must believe that he exists and that he rewards those who earnestly seek him"* (Hebrews 11:6). God is clearly a giver and He will not go back on His Word.

Only God Can Heal

It's been said that "Time heals all wounds," but that saying is not biblical. Many people are still angry, isolated, and getting more and more bitter as the years roll on. The reality is this, time can remove some of the intensity, but only God can heal. God sent His Son Jesus to give us life, and to give it more abundantly (see John 10:10).

In life you will get depressed and have difficult times, and you need to have something stronger in your life to get you through. Your loving Savior Jesus promises to lead and guide you, to never leave you, to make all things work together for good, and to walk with you hand in hand each day of your life until He walks you into eternity with Him—the forever home for which you were created. And then you will be reunited with all those loved ones who preceded you to Heaven.

2. Discouragement

Another way I see satan attacking Christians is with discouragement.

Satan uses discouragement to get you into a mental, emotional, and even physical space where you don't trust God or believe that He has good plans for you.

Remember the baggage example in an earlier chapter? When what you hoped for is delayed, denied, or destroyed, you will definitely feel discouraged. It happens to every Christian, so understand that you are not alone when you feel it.

Sometimes you become discouraged with God because you want what others have. How do you handle it when you don't get your way? You may have been passed over for a job promotion. You may have watched as another family moved into the house you prayed over. That car you sowed a seed on, you just saw it being driven off the dealer's lot.

Let's say it's Monday morning at 7:45 and you can't find those car keys, *again*, and just last week your boss told you, "If you're late one more time, don't even bother showing up!" You may get angry with God. You may have mumbled to yourself as you kicked the cat, "Lord, why does this always happen to me?" It's unrealistic that God is responsible for this situation—did God come down and hide your keys while you slept?

Satan's main goal is to destroy your faith. When he messes things up, he's only too happy to point an accusing finger at God—the only answer to your problems. If you don't recognize that satan is working hard to counter God's good plans for your life, you can easily find yourself so discouraged and angry with God that when you desperately need to go to Him, you don't. This is true discouragement.

Have you dwelt on a problem so much that it eats away at you? That's how satan traps you into discouragement. He makes you focus on what's not going right so that you refuse to see all the good that God is doing or has done in your life.

Think of the apostle Paul again; do you think he was discouraged as he was begging God to deliver him from the thorn in his flesh? Of course he was. Who wants a satanic messenger that torments you?

> *Because of these surpassingly great revelations. Therefore, in order to keep me from becoming conceited, I was given a thorn in my flesh, a messenger of Satan, to torment me. Three times I pleaded with the Lord to take it away from me. But he said to me, "My grace is sufficient for you, for my power is made perfect in weakness." Therefore I will boast all the more gladly about my weaknesses, so that Christ's power may*

rest on me. That is why, for Christ's sake, I delight in weaknesses, in insults, in hardships, in persecutions, in difficulties. For when I am weak, then I am strong (2 Corinthians 12:7-10).

Paul pleaded "three times." You can imagine how this unanswered prayer frustrated Paul. He was used to seeing the Lord move through him when he prayed for others. The Lord's message to Paul: Even though you're a mature apostle, you are still vulnerable to pride. The thorns are there to protect you from yourself.

We see in verse 10 that Paul was able to accept God's answer, even though it wasn't what he wanted to hear. He was able to believe that God really could use this weakness for His benefit and it no longer held him in bondage.

> We can't see God's plan unless we look with the eyes of faith.

God can use something you despise about yourself to keep you humble, especially when He has a purpose for your life like he did for Paul.

But God isn't the only one who has a purpose for you; satan also has a plan for your life, which is to steal, kill, and destroy (see John 10:10). When we're reeling from discouragement, it's easiest to focus on satan's plan because it's right before our eyes. In these situations we can't see God's plan unless we look with the eyes of faith.

Mark Twain said, "Faith is believing something you know ain't true."[3] But's that not what the verse says. It says, *"Now faith is the assurance that what we hope for will come about and the certainty that what we cannot see exists"* (Hebrews 11:1 ISV). How do we look with the eyes of faith? By *"keeping our eyes on Jesus, the champion who initiates and perfects our faith"* (Hebrews 12:2 NLT). This is where eyes of faith look—at Jesus who perfects us.

There's a reason it's called "exercising" your faith. You have to work at it. Growing that faith muscle is like putting a seed in the ground. You have to believe the seed is there even though you can't see it. Certainly don't dig it up to check.

What do you do while you're waiting for it to germinate? Pray without ceasing. Constantly challenge doubt. Study the Word and speak with confidence. Believe you shall receive it and it will manifest. Faith keeps its eyes on Jesus. It believes the invisible until it comes into the visible realm.

3. Exhaustion

A third area I see satan using to attack Christians is in the area of exhaustion.

> Researchers at Washington University School of Medicine in St. Louis bred insomniac flies...that spent only an hour a day asleep.... These insomniac flies lost their balance more often, were slower learners and gained more fat all resembling symptoms that also occur in sleep-deprived humans.[4]

Physical exhaustion can have natural causes. It can happen because we don't understand our limitations, from not getting enough sleep, working too much, or just saying yes to too many commitments. But these can all have a spiritual component, too.

All of these can spring from jealousy and coveting what someone else has. We have to understand we are people who have limits.

Limitations

Each one of us is created in God's image, but that doesn't mean we can do everything. Even God rested on the Sabbath after creating the world and everything in it (see Genesis 2:1-3). He didn't take a day off because He was tired. He took a day to enjoy what He had made. By doing so, He showed us that we need to step back from our work and enjoy what we've labored for.

In order for us to avoid getting burned out, it is vital that we understand our limits and put boundaries in place. Do you overextend yourself or feel like you always have to give more than what you have? We want to please those around us, so we say yes and become more and more exhausted in the process. It is a vicious cycle from which we need to break free.

Saying yes to someone's request when God hasn't asked you to can lead to burnout.

It is important to remember that you control your time. If you don't have good boundaries set in place, you can become physically, emotionally, or mentally exhausted. When exhaustion sets in, you become irritable and less patient with those around you.

For example, say you're a single mom who takes care of four kids, cleans the house, holds down a full-time job, and shuttles the kids back and forth. You are already maxed out, so saying *yes* to someone's request when God hasn't asked you to can lead to burnout.

Sometimes it's fun stuff. Instead of spending time with God, we go to a superficial event, dancing, or drinking, so we feel picked back up. Then we're left with the guilt and shame to go along with our depression. We don't need to struggle with that too.

Sometimes we are jealous of important or busy people, so we fill our calendars to make ourselves appear important and busy. We communicate electronically (emails, social media, text messages, etc.) with too many people and we have a pile of work that we'll never catch up on at the office. Or, we want to keep up with our neighbors. But now our blood pressure is through the roof, and we wonder, *Why am I so tired and depressed all the time?* We wanted to look important and ended up doing what God never asked us to do. God never called us to be like everyone else; He calls us to carry our own load.

Some years ago I became so physically exhausted that I just wanted to give up. When you're a pastor, everyone wants a piece of your time. I ended up being there for everyone but no one knew I was broken down, tired, and worn out. When the weight of the world is on you to be there for everyone else, it's hard to say, "I need help." People assume you don't have faith if you're tired. I had to learn to set boundaries so that I wouldn't burn out.

Thanks to T.D. Jakes and Harry Lee Sewell who helped me see that I wasn't abnormal to feel burned out. It was a season and it was normal. (They actually encouraged me to write this book.)

Some of the most successful people I know are also the most depressed. When people find out how good they are at their business, then everyone wants them. Being good at something is a blessing from God; but until we learn to train others and delegate, we're going to wear ourselves out.

Worn Out

At the end of a long day, we want to come home and just sit on the couch, soaking up the silence. That is not depression. That is part of the natural restoration process after working all day. But, some of us have been feeling poorly for years, wondering why our pendulum is not moving. We continually search our hearts, crying out to God, and looking for answers on every episode of Dr. Phil. We assume that something is off on the inside. But there is nothing wrong with us, spiritually speaking, we are depressed because we are just "plain ole worn out."

Some of us have been so exhausted that we are in a pit of depression, wondering, *Why can't anything ever go in my favor?* It is hard enough just to get through the things we have to do every day, let alone the things we want to do. In this situation the word *no* can become our best friend.

Setting Boundaries

The first step in setting a healthy boundary is identifying what you need. After you decide what you want, then state your boundary. Keep it brief. Be firm, not unkind, but firm. Remember, you aren't responsible for the person's response and you don't have to justify, explain, or apologize.

If learning boundaries is a new skill for you, then be patient with yourself. Learning anything new is a process.

Cast Your Cares on Him

Take heart, God knows where you are in your mental and emotional stability. He knows how much you can bear, and He requests that you cast your burdens on Him. Psalm 55:22 says, *"Cast your cares on the Lord and he will sustain you; he will never let the righteous be shaken."*

Notice that the first step is ours. We need to cast our burdens, or baggage, on Him and He'll carry what is too heavy for us.

Jesus was using a fishing term when he said to "cast" our cares, like those who cast their nets into the sea. When we cast our sorrows on Him we surrender them and we depend on Him to deliver us. Then trust that if the answer doesn't come immediately, He will sustain us until it does.

What I Really Want You to Remember

Because you have a relentless enemy who is after you, you will experience negative life events. You are not to blame for these. Sometimes we contribute to our pain by making poor lifestyle choices. All choices come with consequences. The Prodigal Son and Jonah are great examples of this. Being fully informed before we make decisions can help us avoid negative consequences. God's heart is tender and compassionate toward you. Loss, discouragement, and exhaustion are three things the enemy effectively uses against us. The Lord's solution for this time of heaviness is His invitation for you to cast all your cares upon Him. He is strong enough to carry the load. You were not designed to do so.

APPLICATION EXERCISE

1. Evaluate the intensity of your current loss on a scale from 1-10.

   _____

   _____

2. Pray and ask the Lord to deliver you from this challenging season.

   _____

   _____

3. Cast these cares upon the Lord.

   _____

   _____

4. Remember times when He has moved on your behalf and write them here.

   _____

   _____

5. Write the two words from Psalm 103:12-14 that describe God's attitude toward you. Think about these through the week.

   _____

   _____

Remember, if the worries start again it's because you've taken your cares back and are carrying them by yourself again. If that happens, start over again at Question 2.

SCRIPTURE MEDITATION

Cast your cares on the Lord and he will sustain you; he will never let the righteous be shaken (Psalm 55:22).

WISDOM FROM THE RICK-TION-ARY

"Remember that God wants you to make it even more than you do." (8/5/02)

PRAYER

Lord, I thank You for the understanding that seasons come and go and that this is normal. Help me to remember this when I get discouraged. I also thank You that You personally invite me to cast my cares upon You. I acknowledge that these struggles are too much for me. I thank You that nothing is too big for You and that nothing surprises You. I am grateful that You already have a plan for my healing in this situation. Help me to remember that You are tender and compassionate toward me, even in my weaknesses. I commit myself to partner with You during this challenging time.

VIDEO LINK

www.RICKIERUSH.com/ThePendulum-Ch7

ENDNOTES

1. "Quotations of Perspective," The Quote Garden, http://www.quotegarden.com/perspective.html(accessed 8/12/14).

2.   Ibid.

3.   "Mark Twain," Quote World, http://www.quoteworld.org/ quotes/10293 (accessed 8/12/14).

4.   Linda Thrasybule, "7 Strange Facts About Insomnia," Live Science, http:// www.livescience.com/36454-strange-insomnia -facts-treatments.html (accessed 8/12/14).

Chapter 8

IT'S TIME FOR A REALITY CHECK

This chapter may expose things about yourself that
you weren't aware of. But rejoice, the first step
to healing is understanding there is a problem.

The expression "no pain, no gain," suggests that a season of pain will result in a season of profit. Pain often tells us that something is out of order and needs attention. If my big toe didn't throb when I stubbed it on the table while negotiating my way to snag a midnight snack, then how would I ever know something was wrong with it? In that regard, pain is our friend, signaling to us that something needs attention.

Even though it took me a while, I finally stopped praying to avoid pain. While it is not pleasant, pain lets me know that I need to be set right in some area. But even though it's a healthy indicator,

I still don't want to get stuck in it, because pain is not supposed to last. We're supposed to figure out the source and fix it. We don't want to get stuck in the dumps too long. It's meant to pass.

TALK IS NOT CHEAP—IT'S VITAL

One of satan's most effective and destructive lies is, "You have to hide your problems." Because no one talks about it, we think we're alone in our struggle, which means we don't seek help, accountability, counsel, or prayer. Depression is addressed so little and so poorly in the Christian community that some may think it is the unpardonable sin. Really? Where did we get that idea?

I shared a series of sermons a few years ago on the subject of depression. Two different people who were watching over the Internet called within a day of each other and told me their mothers had sunk into despair and didn't talk about it. No one realized they were depressed until it was too late. Sadly, both women committed suicide the same weekend. The hopeless sadness and depression whispered the lie, "Give up. There's no help for you."

Most people who are feeling hopeless know it; they don't need to be convinced. Rather, they need to be convinced that it is okay to talk about it. You can't defeat heavyheartedness on your own; you need the help of other people in order to get past it.

Note: Ironically, upon my last day of writing this book, I heard the news of an untimely death. A major influence in my life committed suicide from depression. He was not a preacher or a poet, not a teacher or politician—but a comedian who inspired and encouraged me that it was okay to laugh through difficult times. That same comedian took his life. How did his pendulum get stuck? When did his pendulum get stuck? And did anyone notice? His death is another tragic example of why we need to talk about our problems. A smile doesn't always mean people are happy, laughing doesn't always mean it's funny, and helping someone else up does not mean that you aren't down. Be encouraged, you're not alone in your depression—your ending will be better.

A Season of Discouragement Isn't a Sin

Some people might consider discouragement to be a sin. Other equally misinformed people would falsely accuse hidden sin as the cause. Of course when spiritual counsel can't identify the "hidden sin," or when prayer doesn't fix the situation, people face self-condemnation and deeper depression. *What is wrong with me? I'm such a failure.* They spiral deeper and deeper into despair, helped along by fellow well-meaning but misinformed Christians.

Because of this misunderstanding some Christians hesitate to seek professional help. I want to challenge that false belief here and now. If your reactive depression has turned into clinical depression, it is wise to seek help, even if it looks different from what you'd prefer.

Here's a story to help illustrate: A man is sitting on his porch as flood waters rise. A woman floats by in a boat. "Do you need help?" she asks. "No, thanks. I'm trusting in the Lord," says the man. The waters continue to rise. The man retreats upstairs. A raft full of people floats by his second-story window. "Get in. There's plenty of room," someone calls out. "No, thanks," says the man, "I'm trusting in the Lord." The flood waters keep rising. The man is forced to climb to his roof. A helicopter swoops in, lowering its ladder. "Thanks anyway," shouts the man, "I'm trusting in the Lord." Finally he is swept away and drowns. When he gets to Heaven the man asks God, "Why didn't You save me?" "What do you mean," replies God, "I sent two boats and a helicopter."

Sometimes God works in ways we don't expect or prefer—like through doctors.

One component of clinical depression is a chemical imbalance in the brain. People should not be ashamed of taking antidepressant medicine to help balance their brain chemicals, which is similar to a diabetic taking insulin.

Find competent, professional help with your doctor or a psychiatrist while you believe God for your healing and follow the other steps in this book. Don't perish in a flood of depression because you think your deliverance should look more spiritual than a boat, helicopter, or a doctor.

LITTLE THINGS MEAN A LOT

Remember, satan does not move in all his baggage and fill us with sadness overnight. Discouragement creeps in little by little as we get behind on paying the bills and then the repo man comes for our car so we can't get to work, and then we end up losing our job. Then we can't pay for our house, let alone buy decent clothes to look for another job, etc. It's a downward spiral. A little bit of depression comes in with each negative circumstance, making it harder and harder to deal with the next crisis. Although they may be small, these negative circumstances grow, sinking us further and further into the pit of depression.

The good news is that if we are willing, we have the ability to understand the symptoms, the causes, and the necessary treatment. That's why the Lord gives us signs to help us know we're temporarily off balance.

If you've heard me preach, you know I like to frequently make my points using humor—because some things you just have to laugh your way through. Sometimes the way I have given myself comfort is to find the humor in it. This book is no different. I'm not Jeff Foxworthy who became famous for his "You might be a redneck" style of hilarity, but I do feel it's time for a little humor:

You might be depressed if you...

- end up with dreadlocks by accident.
- pray for patience in the drive-thru.
- volunteer at a funeral home.
- watch TV when it's turned off.
- have a screensaver of your ex-wife.
- wear headphones with no music.
- call customer service just to talk.
- you haven't bathed in 14 days.
- are divorced and still wear a wedding ring.
- want a black cat so badly that you spray paint your white one.
- have the winning lotto ticket but are too tired to cash it.

- watch a war movie and think it's a comedy.

- haven't brushed your teeth for a week.

- wake up and the time on your clock is irrelevant.

- haven't interacted with your washer or dryer for 17 weeks.

- have taken up gardening in your bathtub.

- make it to work in time for your lunch break and your boss sees it as an improvement.

- can't talk to yourself because your breath is so bad.

- have heard your spouse say, "Move the empty pizza boxes, I want to go to bed."

- get irritated because your shadow's following you.

- are trying to finance a tattoo.

- know every fast-food employee within 8 square miles and they know your name and your order.

- consider Judge Judy your very best friend in the whole wide world.

- have ever been involved in a fistfight at a little league game.

- wear the same outfit to church, the store, and to bed.

- think the best Sunday dinner is beef jerky, moon pies, and uncooked ramen noodles.

- are tempted to write your number on a bathroom walls just for a chance to chat on the phone.

- think Wall Street should recommend the Hostess snack company buy stock in you.

- consider Jack Daniels as your favorite buddy.

- drove through a car wash with the windows down because you didn't want to get out and clean the inside.

I hope you enjoyed a few chuckles—now back to business.

Through my own experience of hard knocks, counseling others through hard times, and studying the subject from a biblical perspective, I have found eight common signs that indicate an individual could be experiencing some form of reactive depression: moodiness; changes in appetite and sleep pattern; loss of interest in hobbies; a desire for isolation; lack of interest in personal appearance; preoccupation with sad thoughts; and low energy levels. Accurately identifying these signs in our lives is the first step to overcoming them. If we deny our feelings and emotions, we delay our healing.

Let's look in more detail at the eight signs along with some helpful, practical solutions. A later chapter will be dedicated to spiritual solutions.

MOODINESS

One of the first signs that depression is knocking on our door is a significant change in our mood. One extreme is passivity and the other is irritability.

Someone suffering from passivity often won't respond to something that would normally cause an emotional reaction or feeling. A person struggling through a passive phase might be afraid to speak or might show a lack of will or initiative.

The other sign of moodiness is an aggressive behavior. This person interrupts, talks over others, or yells. I'm not talking about being a little irritable after a long day at work and snapping at the kids. I'm talking about going through a week or two of irritability. I'm referring to periods of up to six months in which we are constantly irritated or just plain passive. If we are to come through life swinging, we have to learn to be aggressive when we need to be and passive when it is required. When depression strikes, it usually causes us to reverse those issues—irritable when things should not bother us and passive when we should be fighting for something.

The people around us can usually tell that we're being moody before we recognize it. Our spouses could easily tell us, are probably hoping, and yea, praying for us to be brave enough to ask. If you suspect that you're battling moodiness, perhaps it is time to take a deep breath and ask, "Have you noticed any changes in my mood lately?"

Solutions for Moodiness

If you're struggling with your moods, try the following:

- Learn how to identify the signs of arousal that precede a mood swing and stop it before it starts.

- Recognize negative thoughts and replace them with positive ones.

- Slow down your breathing to calm your mood.

- Identify stressors in your life and try to resolve them.

- Soothing music can help.

- Exercise to start your endorphins (good hormones) flowing—swimming, dancing or a brisk walk.

- Chemical disruptors can also contribute, so avoid perfumes.

- Make time to do the things you love, whether it's relaxing with a good book or pursuing a favorite hobby.

- Get your life in order; getting rid of clutter can reduce your overall stress and help you manage midlife challenges.

- Reduce your stress with massage.[1]

Also, some herbs and aromatherapy help in dealing with mood swings.[2]

Those who are deficient in certain vitamins and other nutrients may notice mood improvement upon increasing their intake of vitamin D and B12, Folic Acid, or Niacin.[3]

Vitamin D For Depression

Low vitamin D levels predispose you to depression. Your doctor can easily perform a lab test to show your vitamin D level. Having a level below 20 ng/mL may raise your risk for depression by 85 percent, compared to having a vitamin D level greater than 30 ng/mL. Vitamin D deficiency occurs more often in African-Americans, city dwellers, the obese, and those suffering from depression.

One way to increase your Vitamin D level is through safe exposure to the sun. Check with your family physician or use a smartphone app to tell you how much UV radiation you're getting and how many IUs of vitamin D you're making based on your local weather conditions, skin tone and age. Your physician will also tell you when to get out of the sun, to protect yourself from sunburn.[4] Vitamin D supplements are also available inexpensively over the counter.

Be sure to do your research using reputable sources, and *always* check with your doctor before starting any vitamin protocol.

APPETITE CHANGES

A second common sign of going through depression is a change in appetite. Some people have a loss, while others have an increase. This can be triggered by emotional eating, which has nothing to do with being hungry.

According to an expert at Remuda Ranch, an eating disorder treatment center in Wickenburg, Arizona, "Emotional eating is eating in response to emotional hunger. When patients eat in response to their emotions, they are soothed by the food as it changes the chemical balance in the brain, produces a feeling of fullness that is more comfortable than an empty stomach, and improves mood through positive association with happier times."[5]

There's a reason why some foods are described as "comfort foods." Sometimes, a person's desires for types of food can change. Health nuts may begin to crave chips and sodas. However, I can testify that my junk food tendencies have not developed into an insatiable craving for kale chips and bean sprouts.

Help for Appetite Changes

While no diet can beat depression, research shows that some diets are better than others. The following tips may help.

Adapt a healthier eating regimen. There is some research to support that a Mediterranean-style diet, which is high in fruits, nuts, legumes, and olive oil, and low in saturated fats, decreases the risk of depression.

Omega-3 fatty acids. These substances...have been shown to be important in brain function. Some studies show that they may enhance a person's response to antidepressant medications.

Vitamins and nutrients. Research shows that deficiency of nutrients such as vitamin B12, vitamin B6, and tryptophan can have a negative effect on mood. Consequently, poor nutrition that results from loss of appetite can further exacerbate depression.

Nutritional support. A dietitian can help someone with depression by creating a nutritionally balanced meal plan that takes into account the patient's individual needs. People with severe depression who experience a loss of appetite may need nutritional supplements to help prevent weight loss and nutrient deficiency.[6]

If you perhaps recognize yourself in this situation, I recommend you check out a hospital support group for those with emotional issues or Emotions Anonymous. Also, when you know what situations and emotions prompt you to eat, you can come up with ways to steer clear of those traps. These food triggers typically fall into five categories.

1. *Social*. Eating when around other people....being encouraged by others to eat; eating to fit in....

2. *Emotional*. Eating in response to boredom, stress, fatigue, tension, depression, anger, anxiety, or loneliness as a way to "fill the void."

3. *Situational*. Eating because the opportunity is there... seeing an advertisement for a particular food, passing by a bakery. Eating may also be associated with certain activities such as watching TV, going to the movies or a sporting event, etc.

4. *Thoughts*. Eating as a result of negative self-worth or making excuses for eating. For example, scolding oneself for how they look or a lack of willpower.

5. *Physiological*. Eating in response to physical cues. For example, increased hunger due to skipping a meal or eating to cure headaches or other pain.[7]

Other ways to combat appetite issues: Remove temptations from your kitchen, keep a journal, distract yourself, cook something healthy, take stock of your emotions and exercise.[8] Don't forget to reward yourself as you achieve even the smallest step. Each time you pat yourself on the back you increase the chances that you'll keep going with your new habits.

CHANGES IN SLEEP PATTERNS

A third common sign of depression is a change in our sleep patterns. I know some guys who end up sleeping on the couch because they thought they were right when their wives were—but that's not what I'm talking about here.

Recent studies show that insomnia often precedes depression.[9] Sleep patterns begin to change in unhealthy ways. Fifteen per cent of depressed people sleep too much.[10] They may start staying up late, watching television, or checking email. Then the next morning they want to sleep instead of go to work.

Others are affected just the opposite. At least 80 percent of depressed people have problems falling asleep or staying asleep.[11] Waking early in the morning and not being able to fall back to sleep and waking up tired are also common. Depression affects how long you sleep, how well you sleep, and whether you wake up in the morning feeling exhausted or refreshed. If you're normally an energetic and healthy person, then you suddenly want to be in bed all day, beware.

A Good Night's Sleep

According to the American Sleep Association, to promote good sleep:

- Maintain a regular sleep routine. Go to bed at the same time. Wake up at the same time.

- Avoid naps if possible. When we take naps, it decreases the amount of sleep that we need the next night—which may cause sleep fragmentation

and difficulty initiating sleep, and may lead to
insomnia.

- Don't stay in bed awake for more than 5-10
minutes. If you find your mind racing, or worrying about not being able to sleep during the
middle of the night, get out of bed, and sit in a
chair in the dark...then return to bed.

- Don't watch TV or read in bed. When you watch
TV or read in bed, you associate the bed with
wakefulness.

- Do not drink caffeine inappropriately. The effects
of caffeine may last for several hours after inges-
tion. ...Remember that soda and tea contain caffeine as well.

- Avoid inappropriate substances that interfere
with sleep. Cigarettes, alcohol, and over-the-
counter medications may cause fragmented sleep.

- Exercise regularly. Exercise before 2 p.m. every
day. ...Avoid rigorous exercise before bedtime.

- Have a quiet, comfortable bedroom. Set your
bedroom thermostat at a comfortable tempera-
ture. ...Your bedroom should be dark. Turn off
bright lights.

- Have a comfortable routine. A warm bath,
shower, meditation, or quiet time.[12]

LOSS OF INTEREST IN HOBBIES

A fourth common sign that we're struggling with some form of depression is that there's a loss of interest or pleasure in things we normally enjoy—exercise, hobbies, music, marital intimacy, or social interactions.

Maybe some of us sew and make quilts as a hobby, but now we'd rather just lie under a quilt and watch television all day. Loss of interest affects our desires. If this happens, you could be going through some downtime in this season.

Help for Loss of Interest

The following suggestions are taken from an informative website and apply to everyone who has experienced or is experiencing a loss, health problem, or other life-changing event.

- Walk, jog, or work out: Physical activity can improve your mood and help you sleep better.

- Eat healthy meals regularly: Good nutrition helps your body and your mind.

- Try to get a good night's sleep: Getting quality sleep can help you feel better.

- Practice relaxation or grounding techniques: A shower, deep breathing, or time in a quiet place to collect your thoughts can help relieve stress and get you through difficult moments.

- Visit a friend: Spending some time with friends can lift your spirits.

- Try to plan some sort of pleasurable activity at least once a day, even if it's something small and even if you aren't sure whether you will enjoy it or not.

Talking to your family and friends about what you're feeling can be a first step. They may be able to provide support and help you discover what might be causing you to lose interest in the things you once enjoyed.[13]

A DESIRE FOR ISOLATION

We may be people who love helping others and love talking to them about what is happening in their lives, but when depression hits, we watch the caller ID carefully before answering. This is an unhealthy withdrawal into oneself.

A desire for isolation is the most common sign of depression and the exact opposite of what we need. According to Stephen Ilardi, PhD, associate professor of psychology at the University of Kansas, "Social withdrawal amplifies the brain's stress response. Social contact helps put the brakes on it."[14]

Sometimes we seek to be alone because we think we are the only ones going through these problems. If we would just stay in community, then we'd know that isn't true and that we don't have to cover up with an act.

Get Out There

I came across an article to share with you that has many valuable and helpful tips to stop self-isolation including:

- Make a plan to call at least one person per day for one week.

- Invite someone over to watch a special television show with you, to have dinner together or play a board game.

- Exercise is a known antidepressant that can help relieve symptoms of depression.

- Volunteering gives you access to a cause you are passionate about, and you can meet others who share your interest.

- Join a group of like-minded people, a support group for people who self-isolate, or a group based on a hobby such as horseback riding, hiking, or a book club.

- Meet someone for coffee and then run errands together.

- Join a few friends to see a movie in the theater.[15]

LACK OF INTEREST IN PERSONAL APPEARANCE

Another common sign of depression is a loss of interest in our personal appearance. I'm not advocating suits and ties every day, but we should care about how we look. I'm also not suggesting you are depressed if you wear a running suit every day, if it's appropriate work attire.

But people struggling with this issue can often go days without putting on deodorant, shaving, dressing well, showering, combing their hair, or even brushing their teeth. They lack the motivation and energy to do these basic habits. I am not talking about having a bad hair day, but I am talking about going to Walmart at 4 p.m. wearing pajamas and hair rollers.

Practical Ways to Rejuvenate Appearance

> Make sure you're hitting all the basics: brush your teeth, use deodorant, wash your clothes regularly, get a haircut, shave, dress appropriately. If you want to go a little further, learn to pamper or spoil yourself: buy a new grooming gadget, use bath salts, create a relaxing atmosphere with music and lighting. ...Learning to take care of yourself is...just another piece of the puzzle toward learning to manage your symptoms and maybe finding a little hope or happiness along the way....[16]

PREOCCUPATION WITH SAD THOUGHTS

The word "ruminate" derives from the Latin word for chewing cud, which is part of a cow's digestive process when it grinds up and swallows food, then regurgitates it later to chew it again. Unfortunately, humans can do the same things with their negative thoughts. We may swallow them, only to realize that three hours later, or 30 seconds later, we're replaying them again in our minds.

> Ruminating about the darker side of life can fuel depression...impair thinking and problem-solving, and drive away critical social support. Such depressive rumination most often occurs in women as a reaction to sadness.... Men, by comparison, more often focus on their emotions when they're angry, rather than sad....[17]

Death and grief are normal, but when we are preoccupied with sad thoughts, then everything in life can seem sad. Bad things happen to good people. But if you can't let go of them over time and through the process of forgiveness, and if you continually rehearse the circumstances over and over in your mind, then it could be a sign that you are suffering with reactive depression.

Use Distraction

Distraction techniques are suggested by Yale University psychologist Susan Nolen-Hoeksema, PhD:

> Practically speaking, people can use such distraction techniques as meditation and prayer to help break the rumination cycle. Other cycle breakers include:
>
> - Taking small actions to begin solving problems.
>
> - Reappraising negative perceptions of events and high expectations of others.
>
> - Letting go of unhealthy or unattainable goals and developing multiple sources of self-esteem.
>
> For example, women who build their identity solely around family are rumination-prone because they've got all of their self-esteem and social support in one basket. So helping them to develop multiple sources of gratification and social support can be helpful buffers against stressful events in any one of those domains.[18]

Also, if you reside in a world of soap operas or non-edifying music and TV, you need to make some drastic changes. The world of 24-hours-a-day news coverage of the latest political scandal, war, and horrific crime helps to ensure a preoccupation with sad and negative thoughts.

LOW ENERGY LEVELS

Finally, the last common sign of depression is experiencing low energy levels. All of a sudden we hit a wall and just burn out. Our energy levels seem to have evaporated along with our motivation. It's like all of our natural vitality drained away and we're left with a mere shadow of who we once were.

You may feel as if you've just jogged a marathon; but in reality, you spent the evening on the couch watching a movie marathon. Low energy levels leave us tired, lethargic, and make us appear lazy. You can be ready to take a nap again, just from the effort it takes to extricate yourself from the bed each morning. You may get sleepy while sleeping.

Please, don't get me wrong here. When you get off work tomorrow and are tired from the day's efforts, that's not dysfunctional. That is just called being sleepy or physically exhausted. It's not the same as having consistent low energy levels from reactive depression.

OVERCOMING DEPRESSION—
TAKE IT ONE STEP AT A TIME

Before making any change, assess where you are now and what is a reasonable goal. If people are so depressed that they stay in bed all day, a good goal for them is to get up and take a shower. For other people who are also depressed but make it to work, their goal might be to engage in one pleasurable activity per day.

Also, remember that making a small *stretch* is a step in the right direction. Some people berate themselves because taking a shower is a seemingly trivial target. But remember that it leads to another step, which leads to another step. All these steps are simply the building blocks to getting better.[19]

I know I've mentioned the importance of exercise before, but I want to quote from a scientific study that had stunning results regarding exercise and depression:

> It has been established that excess sitting may lead to physical health problems, but studies show it may harm your mental health as well. [In a study of middle-aged] women who sat more than seven hours a day were found to have a 47 percent higher risk of depression than women who sat four hours or less per day. Women who didn't participate in ANY physical activity had a *99 percent* higher risk of developing depression than women who exercised. The findings were crystal clear: excessive sitting and lack of exercise resulted in an increase in depression symptoms among middle-aged women.
>
> Researchers concluded that increased physical activity could alleviate existing depression symptoms and possibly even prevent future symptoms. And reducing the amount of daily sitting time may relieve existing symptoms of depression. The key to minimizing the effects of

sitting is to stand up often, optimally every 15 minutes, and perform a different exercise for 30-60 seconds.[20]

Additional Symptoms

Additional symptoms of reactive depression include: pain or bellyaches not responding to treatment, headaches, memory problems, sadness, difficulty making decisions, thoughts of suicide or death, excessive crying, weight changes, persistent anxiety and feeling of emptiness, guilt, hopelessness, helplessness and pessimism, problems with sex drive, rapid heart beat drug and alcohol abuse.[21]

> Women who don't exercise have a 99 percent higher risk of developing depression than women who exercise.

MAKING A PIT STOP

It is quite common to hear people talking about "feeling in the pits." If you're a NASCAR fan you know what a pit stop is. Although pit stops are necessary to keep the race cars functioning at peak capacity, the goal is to get in and out as quickly as possible. No one sets up a barbeque grill or brings in a masseuse for the driver. That would be a very misdirected pit crew.

Even though we love Jesus with all our hearts and we're doing everything we know to show it, sometimes depression comes and stays too long. The enemy brings depression in order to cripple us, causing us to stop living life to the fullest. He comes to steal, kill, and destroy. But Jesus came so we can have the abundant life He promised (see John 10:10).

Without spiritual intervention—without God's Word applied to our lives by the power of the Holy Spirit—it's impossible for the blues to leave. We must not get stuck there! We've got to be people who press through, trusting God for our ultimate deliverance.

> When experiencing signs of depression, call on Someone able and willing to set you free—your heavenly Father.

Getting free is a partnership between us and God. He has a part and we have a part. He won't do our part and we can't do His. We'll look at specifics later in the book, but be encouraged—remember, the pendulum still swings equally in both directions.

WHAT I REALLY WANT YOU TO REMEMBER

Emotional pain can play a helpful role by letting us know that something is wrong and needs attention. One of the enemy's most destructive lies is that we have to hide our problems. A season of depression is not a sin, nor is it an indication of sin in your life. If we deny our feelings and emotions, we delay our healing. Eight common indicators that we are struggling with depression are: moodiness, appetite changes, changes in sleep patterns, loss of interest in hobbies, desire for isolation, lack of interest in personal appearance, preoccupation with sad thoughts, and low energy levels.

APPLICATION EXERCISE

1. Is there something painful that has stayed too long in your life? What?

    _____

    _____

2. Have you kept it hidden?

    _____

    _____

3. Circle any of the following that you are currently experiencing: Moodiness, Appetite Changes, Changes in Sleep Patterns, Loss of Interest in Hobbies, A Desire for Isolation, A Loss of Interest in Personal Appearance, A Preoccupation with Sad Thoughts, Low Energy Levels.

    _____

    _____

4. Circle anything you are suffering from under the Additional Symptoms paragraph (see page 144).

5. Can you give yourself permission to feel your "negative" emotions? Why is feeling them healthier than denying them?

    _____

    _____

SCRIPTURE MEDITATION

The thief's purpose is to steal and kill and destroy. My purpose is to give them a rich and satisfying life (John 10:10 NLT).

WISDOM FROM THE RICK-TION-ARY

"When you are dealing with God it is always too soon to quit." (11/27/06)

PRAYER

Lord, help me to not deny nor hide these feelings and symptoms that I am experiencing. Sometimes I feel overwhelmed by them and ashamed of them, too. Help me to believe, during this discouraging time, that You have Your loving eyes focused on me. Help me to believe that this season is temporary and that You have good plans for my life. I put my trust in You and continue to cast my cares on You. Help me to do the daily, practical things that will speed my healing.

VIDEO LINK

www.RICKIERUSH.com/ThePendulum-Ch8

ENDNOTES

1. For a complete list of solutions, visit the Women In Balance Institute website at http://womeninbalance.org/symptoms-solutions/irritability-mood-swings/ (accessed 8/13/14).

2. Pooja Luthra, "Mood Swings in Women—Causes & Solutions," Ezine Articles, submitted August 9, 2008, http://ezinearticles .com/?Mood-Swings-in-Women---Causes-and-Solutions& id=1396385 (accessed 8/13/14).

3. Jack Challem, *The Food-Mood Solution* (Hoboken, NJ: John Wiley & Sons, Inc., 2007); http://www.livestrong.com/ article/252146-vitamins-for-moodiness-and-irritability/ (accessed 8/13/14).

4. Dr. Mercola, "Vitamin D for Depression, Dementia, and Diabetes," Mercola.com, http://articles.mercola.com/sites/ articles/archive/2014/08/21/vitamin-d-depression-dementia. aspx?e_cid=20140821Z1_DNL_art_1&utm_source=dnl&utm_ medium=email&utm_content=art1&utm_campaign= 20140821Z1&et_cid=DM54156&et_rid=629832380 (accessed 8/13/14).

5. Chris Iliades, MD, "Depression's Effect on Your Appetite," Everyday Health, http://www.everydayhealth.com/health-report/major-depression/depressions-effect-on-appetite.aspx (accessed 8/13/14).

6. Ibid.

7. WebMD, "Weight Loss: Emotional Eating," MedicineNet.com, http://www.medicinenet.com/emotional_eating/article.htm (accessed 8/13/14).

8. Paraphrased from "Six Ways to Beat Emotional Eating," Everyday Health, http://www.everydayhealth.com/ southbeachdiet/six-ways-to-beat-emotional-eating.aspx#07 (accessed 8/13/14).

9. Peter Jaret, "Depression and Insomnia," WebMD, http://www .webmd.com/depression/features/sleep-problems (accessed 8/13/14).

10. Hara Estroff Marano, "Bedfellows: Insomnia and Depression," *Psychology Today,* July 1, 2003, http://www.psychologytoday.com/articles/200307/bedfellows-insomnia-and-depression (accessed 8/13/14).

11. Ibid.

12. Visit the following website for a more detailed list of the tips: American Sleep Association, "Sleep Hygiene Tips," http://www.sleepassociation.org/index.php?p=sleephygienetips (accessed 8/13/14).

13. "Loss of Interest or Pleasure," Make the Connection, http://maketheconnection.net/symptoms/loss-of-interest (accessed 8/13/14).

14. Jennifer Soong, "6 Common Depression Traps to Avoid," WebMD, http://www.webmd.com/ahrq/depression-traps-and-pitfalls (accessed 8/14/14).

15. Kyra Sheahan, "How to Stop Self-Isolation," eHow, http://www.ehow.com/how_8554135_stop-selfisolation.html (accessed 8/14/14).

16. David Dich, "Personal Appearance and Hygiene," All Things Depression, http://allthingsdepression.com/2011/03/personal-appearance-and-hygiene/ (accessed 8/14/14).

17. Bridget Murray Law, "Probing the depression-rumination ccycle," American Psychological Association 36, no. 10 (2005), http://www.apa.org/monitor/nov05/cycle.aspx (accessed 8/14/14).

18. Ibid.

19. Margarita Tartakovsky, "5 Ideas for Boosting Your Energy When Depression Strikes," Psych Central, http://psychcentral.com/lib/5-ideas-for-boosting-your-energy-when-depression-strikes/0009491 (accessed 8/20/14).

20. Dr. Mercola, "Prolonged Sitting Can Lead to Depression and Other Mental Health Problems," Mercola.com, http://articles .mercola.com/sites/articles/archive/2014/08/07/prolonged-sitting -depression.aspx?e_cid=20140807Z1_DNL_art_1&utm _source=dnl&utm_medium=email&utm_content=art1&utm _campaign=20140807Z1&et_cid=DM54831&et_rid=613748364 (accessed 8/14/14).

21. "Reactive Depression. What is it?"; http://www.depressionhelps .com/reactive-depression-what-is-it/ (accessed 8/14/14).

Chapter 9

IT'S TIME TO TAKE DOWN DENIAL

In the cartoon strip Calvin and Hobbes, the young boy Calvin is asked, "What state do you live in?" His response is quite sophisticated: "Denial."[1] We should all be so honest!

Spiritual deflation is serious. It's not to be taken lightly because you *really, really* have a literal enemy and he *really, really* wants to destroy you. The symptoms listed in the previous chapter are satan's strongholds. When you acknowledge to yourself and others that you are in the midst of difficult times, winning your battle becomes easier. Eventually your pendulum will swing back to a time of joy, but it takes time and effort. Breaking agreement with denial is the first step to come out of your corner swinging.

Let's look at three steps you must take:

1. You must acknowledge to yourself and accept that you are experiencing difficult times.

2. You must acknowledge to God that you desire to be delivered.

3. You must acknowledge your need for healing to others.

ADMIT AND ACCEPT THAT YOU ARE EXPERIENCING DIFFICULT TIMES

Here's a little story about denial. It might sound familiar, but be assured that it's not about you; but if you can find yourself in the story, then by all means use it to help come through your difficult time.

There's a young man, about 30, who has experienced a lot of ups and downs. From a young age he started drinking. Soon his alcohol consumption went from being just a social thing to something he did when he woke up, when he needed to unwind after a long day, and a way to numb his pain. Sometimes he drank until he passed out. His family and friends just saw it as a way of life and they didn't say anything.

He eventually met and married a young woman. She feared that he would drive drunk and kill himself or someone else, but she stopped bringing it up because he became violently angry. She became pregnant and prayed for God to change her husband's taste for alcohol. He just saw it as another way for her to nag him.

One day after work he hit the bar and had drink upon drink until the bartender denied him. He stormed out of the bar and on his way home lost control of the car and hit a tree. Fortunately he didn't die. He was ordered to rehab to avoid jail time.

He attended his first session begrudgingly. He halfheartedly listened to the other people admit that they were there because of their drinking. When it was his turn, he said, "I don't belong here. I like to drink but it's not a problem for anyone." The members smiled at him and a woman stood and said, "Hi, I'm Martha, and I'm an alcoholic." She chuckled to herself. He scoffed because he didn't see the humor in her being a worthless alcoholic.

She continued, "I too was forced to be here because I didn't think my drinking was a problem. When people told me I did, I thought they were judging me. I isolated myself and the only companion I had was my favorite wine. Soon wine wasn't enough for me at home so I would drink at restaurants and bars. One day after an evening out I decided to bathe my six-month-old twin girls...."

You can finish the rest of the story. It wasn't shared to sadden you, it was to show you how denial can cause you greater pain than you realize. Both of these characters refused to admit that they had a problem until it was too late for one and almost too late for the other.

What you may not realize is that satan crept in when you didn't expect it, and he planted seeds of despair, rejection, bitterness, frustration, fear, and other things that have held you for too long. These things grew in dark places in your mind and they manifested at a time when life seemed to be unbearable. You may have lost your job, lost a loved one, become discouraged because of a missed opportunity or are just plain old exhausted from always giving to people. You feel defeated, but you don't believe that you are depressed.

Satan's greatest trick is to keep you in denial and keep you from calling on the name of the Lord. He wants you to believe that what you are going through is too personal, no one else's business, something that you can pull through on your own, not that bad or that, because you are a Christian who loves God with all your heart, you shouldn't be having these problems.

Denial is not your friend.

This is how satan gets you. This is how he keeps you in denial and denying your need for help. He convinces you to reject what you hear at church or from people who love you. The negative self-talk accelerates. Like the man who enjoyed drinking despite his wife's concerns, you continue to move forward, hiding your pain instead of releasing it to God.

ACKNOWLEDGE TO GOD THAT YOU DESIRE TO BE DELIVERED

Refusal to acknowledge your needs means you are operating in spiritual pride. You might say, "I don't need anyone's help. I put myself here and I can get myself out." These are satan's whispered lies. You must come out of agreement with him and cry out to the Lord, telling Him that you are in need.

Find the courage to call on God, even when it *feels* like He has completely abandoned you. Be assured that He has not. He promises in His Word, *"The Lord himself goes before you and will be with you; he will never leave you nor forsake you. Do not be afraid; do not be discouraged"* (Deuteronomy 31:8). He is waiting on you to let Him resolve your issues.

AFTER TWELVE YEARS—HEALING

There was a woman in the Bible who was bleeding for 12 years. She spent all her money on doctors and was finally banished outside the city because she was proclaimed "unclean." Then someone told her about Jesus. Out of desperation she went into the city. A large crowd had surrounded Jesus, obscuring Him from her view. But this did not deter her. She pushed her way through the crowd. When she got close, she dropped to the ground, crawling toward Jesus. She didn't want to ask Him for anything. She didn't want to bother Him. She just wanted to touch the hem of His garment; because she knew if she could do that, she would be healed (see Matthew 9:21). Amid the pushing, shoving, and general confusion, she grabbed the tassel on His clothing as He walked by. Immediately He stopped and searched for the one who had touched Him. Initially the disciples mocked His question, "Who touched Me?" because he was surrounded by scores of people who were all touching and pulling on Him.

> *Peter said, "But Master, we've got crowds of people on our hands. Dozens have touched you." Jesus insisted, "Someone touched me. I felt power discharging from me." When the woman realized that she couldn't*

remain hidden, she knelt trembling before him. In front of all the people, she blurted out her story—why she touched him and how at that same moment she was healed. Jesus said, "Daughter, you took a risk trusting me, and now you're healed and whole. Live well, live blessed!" (Luke 8:45-48 MSG)

Ignoring their scoffing, Jesus addressed His concerns for feeling His divine power being awakened. The woman came forward trembling, admitting that she only wanted to be healed. Being touched by her faith, Jesus acknowledged her healing and blessed her. This was His way of showing those around her that she was no longer an outcast and to be accepted back into the community. Her days of illness and isolation were over.

The Bible gives this woman no name or nationality. She was sick, poor, and had no other resources or hope. All she had was a desire to be healed and she acknowledged, through her actions, that she needed help. That's what you have to do. You may not have an issue of blood, but there is something that is holding you in bondage—and Jesus is passing by. It's your time. Are you going to let Him help?

ACKNOWLEDGE YOUR NEED FOR HEALING TO OTHERS

There is an old movie called *Rocky*. It's about a young man who had hopes of becoming a championship boxer, and his cornerman, Mickey. A cornerman is a coach or someone who assists a fighter during a bout. The cornerman stays in the corner of the ring, outside the combat area during the fight. Because the boxer can't see all that his opposition is doing, he has to have someone watching, warning, teaching him, telling him he's letting his guard down. He cannot tend to all of his wounds and stop his bleeding between rounds. He needs a good cornerman.

Before Rocky had a cornerman he was flailing in life, not living up to his potential. When he was ready to take his career seriously, he sought the assistance of Mickey. Mickey successfully trained prize fighters by not being sympathetic to complainers who wanted to give up. He took what they had to offer and made them true contenders. As Rocky's popularity grew, so did Mickey's intensity and what was required. Mickey pushed Rocky past himself. There were several movie sequels and Rocky eventually became the champion that Mickey saw in him.[2]

WHO IS YOUR MICKEY?

That's the short version of why you need others, but I use it to help you realize that when you get discouraged, you need someone in your corner who is going to push you out of your spiritual deflation. You need someone with whom you can honestly share your actions and motives. Who is that person you run from because you don't want to hear the truth? Who never accepts invitations to your pity parties? Who just won't let you slip away and die silently? Pray that the Lord will allow the right person into your life to help you through this season.

Here are a few dos and a few don'ts when finding your cornerman:

- First, if you're female then your Mickey should be female.

157

- She shouldn't struggle with the same issues you have. For example, two recovering alcoholics can end up being a bad influence on each other.

- Pick someone who will challenge but not condemn you, who will confront you in love.

- What is the person's availability? Can she meet with you once a week at a regular time? Is she available to take a phone call when you need to talk?

- Set expectations. How does she feel she can best help? How do you feel she can best help?

- If you stumble, what do you want her to do?

- Will you give her permission to say what needs to be said without fear of retaliation?

I have two more suggestions when picking a cornerman. Actually, they are about how to avoid a bad one. If you seek counsel with ungodly people, you will reap ungodly advice. The Bible encourages us to seek godly counsel: *"By wise counsel* [guidance] *thou shalt make thy war: and in multitude of counsellors there is safety"* (Proverbs 24:6 AKJV).

There's an old joke about a man who was lying drunk beside a pig. Two women walked by and one said to the other as she turned up her nose, "I've heard it said that 'One is defined by the company one keeps.'" And the pig got up and walked away.

Unfortunately, if the only people you have to talk to are negative, you begin to adopt their negative thoughts as your own.

When you change your thought patterns, you ultimately change how you speak.

The second consideration is this: sometimes our burdens are too heavy for people who are spiritual lightweights. For example, Job's friends and even his wife. They didn't have discernment; they doubted Job's innocence and falsely attributed his tribulations to God, not satan. With friends like that, who needs enemies?

Job's wife encouraged him to "Curse God and die." I always thought it was interesting that satan killed all Job's children and all his livestock and all his servants, but *left Job's wife*. You can see why, can't you? Make sure the people in your corner are strong in faith and love. You don't want to end up with people like Job's friends (or even worse—his wife).

If you don't have someone who can help you, then seek professional help. Not everyone is privileged to have a cornerman; but everyone, including you, deserves to get the help needed to recover from difficult times.

WHAT I REALLY WANT YOU TO REMEMBER

Three necessary steps to breaking free:

1. You must acknowledge to yourself and accept that you are experiencing difficult times.

2. You must acknowledge to God that you desire to be delivered.

3. You must acknowledge your need for healing to others. Rocky couldn't become a champion without Mickey, his good cornerman. We all need a "Mickey" in our corner to speak life into us after we've surrendered to death.

APPLICATION EXERCISE

1. Write down who Mickey is to you or who you hope could be your Mickey.

    _____

    _____

2. If you don't have a Mickey, write the name of your doctor or competent therapist.

    _____

    _____

3. Write down a time that you will contact your Mickey or phone a professional.

    _____

    _____

4. Take a few minutes now and listen to the song, "If I Can Just Touch the Hem of His Garment."[3] Close your eyes and picture yourself, in your desperation, pushing through the crowd, reaching out to Jesus and receiving your healing. (See endnote 3 for link.)

5. In your mind play out this scenario of you triumphing over your issue. Do this several times each day.

SCRIPTURE MEDITATION

The Lord himself goes before you and will be with you; he will never leave you nor forsake you. Do not be afraid; do not be discouraged (Deuteronomy 31:8).

We all have times when we *feel* abandoned by God. Meditate on this verse throughout the week and the thought, *I know that Jesus has never left me at any time; because if He had, the enemy would have taken my life.*

WISDOM FROM THE RICK-TION-ARY

"Jesus keeps hanging around because He knows that we need strength." (4/12/04)

PRAYER

Lord, in the name of Jesus, I come out of agreement with denial and admit that I am spiritually deflated. I admit that I have blocked You out. I admit that I have rejected help because I thought I was fine or that I could do everything on my own. But I can't, Lord. I admit that now and I need You to come into my life, into my spirit, into my mind and renew me. Change me, Lord, and restore me. Bring a cornerman to help in my healing.

VIDEO LINK

www.RICKIERUSH.com/ThePendulum-Ch9

ENDNOTES

1. "Quotes About Denial: Bill Watterson," Good Reads, https://
    www.goodreads.com/quotes/tag/denial; Bill Watterson,
    (accessed 8/14/14).

2. To watch the Rocky movie trailer, visit: http://tinyurl.com/
    o6lmgmr or https://www.youtube.com/watch?v=YgmK7110jYU.

3. To hear "If I Can Just Touch the Hem of His Garment," visit:
    http://tinyurl.com/nzov2fp or https://www.youtube.com/
    watch?v=noSLw7v_kEM.

Chapter 10

It's Time to Declare

Henry Ford said, "Whether you think you can, or you think you can't—you're right." It's just as accurate to say, "Whether you *speak* you can, or *speak* you can't—you're right." Apparently Henry was more than just a car manufacturer; he had some spiritual insight also.

Negative self-talk is automatic. You probably don't even know you're doing it, much less recognize the effect it has on your mood. A positive self-talker might say, "I need to lose 15 pounds. I'll start working out." A negative self-talker might say, "I look like a fat walrus in these jeans. No one will ever love me." Same situation, drastically different responses.

It Begins with a Thought

Negative thoughts are a gateway to depression. That's why the apostle Paul commanded us to be transformed by the renewing

163

of our minds (Romans 12:2). Everything we speak begins with a thought. The only thing that can escape our lips is what's already stored in our minds. Taking our thoughts captive is the way to prevent negative talk. We must choose our thoughts so that our words are uplifting.

Here are some examples of negative self-talk and how you might modify it.

- "I'm terrified of the future" becomes "God promises He has a bright future for me!" (see Jeremiah 29:11).

- "I'm weak. I can't accomplish anything" becomes "I'm so glad God strengthens me!" (see Psalm 89:21).

- "We can't pay the bills this month" becomes "God is our Provider and He meets all our needs!" (see Philippians 4:19).

- "I'm exhausted" becomes *"I am strong!"* (see Joel 3:10).

Jesus said, *"The words I have spoken to you—they are full of the Spirit and life"* (John 6:63). How much of what we speak lines up with God's Word or is of the Sprit and brings life? How much puts us squarely in agreement with the enemy? The thought of siding with the devil is shocking, but unfortunately we do it every day. When we agree with the enemy with our words, we become our own worst enemy and step right into his camp.

THE POWER OF SELF TALK

Self-talk is what we say to ourselves in any given situation. Every person does this all day long, whether positive or negative. Even secular psychologists understand self-talk's natural power. With only the power of our words we can change our mood and our attitude. Unfortunately, for many Christians, negative self-talk takes center stage and immediately causes us to live a life of spiritual deflation.

With self-talk you are either continuously talking yourself out of something or talking yourself further into it. I asked a woman the other day "How are you doing?" Her reply? "I'm trying to get a migraine." I actually flinched. Then I said, "Well if you're trying to get a migraine, you'll no doubt succeed. Why don't you try *not* to get one?"

> **Your mind is a garden, your thoughts are seeds. You can grow flowers, or you can grow weeds.**

On the other hand, you can talk yourself out of things you want as well. Here's another example. There is a job opening that your supervisor suggested you apply for. But your equally qualified co-worker wants the same position. Instead of taking the opportunity and thanking God, you talk yourself out of applying: *He has more confidence. He can think quickly on his feet. I'll probably freeze up when I interview and make a fool of myself.* This lack of confidence also leads to you being overlooked for future promotions. God provided you with an opportunity, but you talked yourself out of it.

This example is almost too close to home for me. When I was in grade school we had to fundraise. I would take a deep breath, and with quivering legs step onto my neighbor's porch. Another deep breath. Knock, knock. Waiting for an answer was miserable. When the door opened, here was my smooth sales pitch: "You don't want to buy any candy, do you?" No one would have predicted back then that I would end up writing a motivational book!

BIBLICAL EXAMPLES

Peter's doubting self-talk limited his time on top of the water. He initially believed that he could walk out to Jesus, but when he saw the waves he panicked. What do you think his self-talk was like? *Hey, I'm walking on water. This is so cool. Wow, I bet John is really jealous. Hey, that's a big wave. That's a bigger wave. I can't withstand these...glub, glub, glub.* His self-talk took him right under. (Do you think John laughed? I bet he did.) Peter did what the other disciples never imagined, but his miracle moment was cut short because he didn't speak words of faith.

Another way we excel at negative self-talk is complaining. The lame man by the pool of Bethesda is a prime example. He was placed there in hopes that when the angel stirred the water, he would be able to get in and be healed. Unfortunately, he never got his chance. That caused him to become bitter and speak out of his pain.

One of the men lying there had been sick for thirty-eight years. When Jesus saw him and knew he had been ill for a long time, he asked him, "Would you like to get well?" "I can't, sir," the sick man said, "for I have no one to put me into the pool when the water bubbles up. Someone else always gets there ahead of me." Jesus told him, "Stand up, pick up your mat, and walk!" (John 5:5-8 NLT)

Jesus asked him, "Do you want to be healed?" You would think that the man who had been there for 38 years would have shouted, "YES, LORD!" Instead he complained about not being able to get in the pool. Jesus didn't walk away because of his complaining; Jesus showed him mercy and grace and granted his healing.

Have you done what this man did? When you know you need help, you complain instead of taking advantage of the opportunity God has for you. Sometimes you will only have a short time to take advantage of a divine opportunity. It's like the job example...you missed the moment because you spoke against it, despite knowing it was what you prayed for.

A Closed Mouth Gathers No Foot

The Bible clearly says that life and death lie in the power of the tongue: *"The tongue can bring death or life; those who love to talk will reap the consequences"* (Proverbs 18:21 NLT). Do you really believe it? If someone listened to you, could they tell you believed it?

Have you considered that you may be experiencing the bad side of the pendulum swing because you spoke those things into existence? If you speak brokenness, you will have brokenness. If you speak unhappiness, then you will have unhappiness. This is not a hard concept. Your words have the power and authority to grow your life or defeat you.

You may see it as "speaking your mind," "telling the truth," or (posturing with hands on hips) "Well I just have to be honest!" but some things just don't need to be said, especially if the things you have to say are negative. Simple enough?

Before you say anything counter to the Bible, think of your tongue as a tornado that comes with no warning and literally destroys everything in its path. Are you tired of your words hurting you and others? If you desire to spare yourself and them, then control the devastation of the pink tornado.

Pity Party for One

Self-talk also opens you up to plan and celebrate your own pity party. There's an old song that says, "It's my party and I'll cry if I want to." When you engage in pity parties you are telling yourself that you deserve to be where you are and that no one can move you from your place of lowliness until you are ready. That's a horrible approach to life, and it's a sure way to miss out on your blessings.

Every negative word you speak can convince you that you don't deserve what God promised you. If you allow negative thoughts to dictate where you are and where you are going, you'll live in a defeated state of mind because you don't feel you qualify for God's mercy. Negative self-talk is oftentimes the main reason Christians enter into a place of spiritual hopelessness.

Even in the midst of bad circumstances we have a choice as to what we think and what we say. If you're told that you are going to lose your job, do you thank God for a better position? Do you accept what you are told instead of immediately rebuking the enemy and his attacks?

If the doctor says you have high blood pressure, do you repeat it instead of speaking your healing? I suggest that as you battle for your healing you say, "I'm fighting high blood pressure." Once you claim it, the devil will make sure it's yours. "My high blood pressure. My migraines. My diabetes...." Don't let these words roll off your lips. I've been sharing about the importance of speaking about our seasons of discouragement. When you speak of it, and I definitely encourage you to do so, don't say, "My depression...," rather say, "In this season I'm fighting depression."

SELF-INFLICTED WOUNDS

Sometimes we have to admit that our attacks are because of what we said. We're not reaping the results of what *he* said or what *she* said...it's what came out of *our* mouth. Sometimes satan can even take a day off because you are doing a wonderful job convincing yourself that you don't deserve anything from God. Your self-talking can even speak louder than God's voice until you eventually stop believing in His promises or His love for you. Negative self-talk makes satan's job very easy.

> **Negative self-talk is a tool that satan leaves behind when you evict him.**

Stop casting satan out of everyone else. Cast him out of yourself! You are filled with the Holy Spirit; you should have no room to receive satan or his thoughts. Do you continue to believe that satan is making you do things when he's just sitting back waiting for you to harvest what he planted in your mind before you halfheartedly rebuked him? It sounds harsh, but you have to *fight!*

Pull out the Scriptures and by faith confess them out loud. Break the negative sound barrier over your life. Don't just speak—make a declaration, sound the charge, this is warfare! You always win over satan's attacks if you control your tongue.

GIVE YOURSELF A GIFT

Long-term studies show that self trash-talk is associated with higher stress levels and even depression.[1] When we experience a personal failure, it's easy to give in to discouragement. But successful people credit their success with their ability to learn quickly from their mistakes. Give yourself a gift—mess up and move on!

Read what Michael Jordan has to say: "I've missed more than 9,000 shots in my career. I've lost almost 300 games. Twenty-six times, I've been trusted to take the game winning shot and missed. I've failed over and over and over again in my life. And that is why I succeed."[2]

WATCH FOR THESE KINDS OF SELF-TALK

The following are four concrete suggestions to help you recognize and overcome negative self-talk:

1. *Self-Limiting Talk*. When we are self-limiting we may say things like, "I can't tell him how I feel" or "It's too hard to finish the project" or "I'm getting so fat!" Self-limiting talk creates a self-fulfilling prophecy because we stop looking for solutions and assume defeat....

2. *Jumping to Conclusions.* When we experience an uncomfortable situation, we make interpretations rather than simply stating the facts. For example, we'll say, "I tried on my jeans and looked so disgusting," or "Tom talked to me and I made a fool of myself...." When we jump to conclusions, we assume the worst and make fact out of what might be fiction.

3. *Habits of Speech.* Our speech patterns can be so automatic that we don't even notice them... "What do you expect from a dumb blonde?" or "I'm so stupid!" Though these detrimental habits may sometimes be disguised as humor, they aren't funny at all.

4. *Others' Thoughts Become Our Own.* Some of our thoughts are planted by external sources such as our parents, spouse, colleagues, or friends. These well-meaning voices have clear expectations of us that become a part of our own self-talk. When others' thoughts become our own we begin to act out of guilt, rather than desire.[3]

The following is an abbreviated list and descriptions of strategies compiled by Elizabeth Scott that can help you become more conscious of your internal dialogue and its content:

1. *Thought-Stopping:* As you notice yourself saying something negative in your mind, you can stop your thought midstream by saying to yourself, "Stop." Saying this aloud will be more powerful, and having

to say it aloud will make you aware of how many times you are stopping negative thoughts, and where.

2. *Rubber-Band Snap:* Another therapeutic trick is to walk around with a rubber band around your wrist; as you notice negative self-talk, pull the band away from your skin and let it snap back. It'll hurt a little, and serve as a slightly negative consequence that will both make you more aware of your thoughts, and help to stop them!

3. *Replace Negative Statements:* A good way to stop a bad habit is to replace it with something better. Once you're aware of your internal dialogue, here are some ways to change it:

   - Milder Wording: Have you ever been to a hospital and noticed how the nurses talk about "discomfort" instead of "pain"? This is generally done because "pain" is a much more powerful word.... You can try this strategy in your daily life. In your self-talk, turning more powerful negative words to more neutral ones can actually help neutralize your experience. Instead of using words like "hate" and "angry" (as in, "I *hate* traffic! It makes me so *angry*!"), you can use words like "don't like" and "annoyed" ("I don't like traffic; it makes me annoyed,") sounds much milder, doesn't it?).

   - Change Negative to Neutral or Positive: As you find yourself mentally complaining about something, rethink your assumptions. Are you assuming something is a negative event when it isn't, necessarily? (For example, having your plans cancelled at the last minute can be seen as a negative, but what you do with your newly-freed schedule can be what you make of it.) The next time you find yourself stressing about something...see if you can come up with a neutral or positive replacement.

- Change Self-Limiting Statements to Questions: Self-limiting statements like "I can't handle this!" or "This is impossible!" are particularly damaging because they increase your stress... *and* they stop you from searching for solutions. The next time you find yourself thinking something that limits the possibilities of a given situation, turn it into a question. Doesn't *"How* can I handle this?" or *"How* is this possible?" sound more hopeful and open up your imagination to new possibilities?[4]

Now you have a good understanding of how detrimental negative self-talk is and you have some practical resources. Stop this negative habit and help your pendulum swing back into the good times when your speaking adds value to your life and to the lives of others.

WHAT I REALLY WANT YOU TO REMEMBER

Self-talk is something we do automatically all day long. It either puts us in alignment with God or the enemy. Our words have power to change our attitude or mood for better or worse. Regardless of the circumstances, we always have a choice as to whether we speak negatively or positively. We should fight negative circumstances with positive words. Negative talking empowers satan. Get serious and cast him out. Learn quickly from your mistakes—mess up and move on. Start implementing these helpful, practical steps today.

APPLICATION EXERCISE

1. How does your speech add value to your life and to others?

   _____

   _____

2. Make an effort to catch your negative self-talk and re-place it with a godly perspective.

3. If you make a mistake, is it the end of the world, or does it prove you're just human?

   _____

   _____

4. Talk to yourself as nicely as you talk to your friends.

5. When someone compliments you this week, don't disagree. The appropriate response is "Thank you."

6. If no one compliments you, compliment yourself. Write it here:

   _____

   _____

7. Write out the following verses. What do they say about the power of our words?

   - Proverbs 10:19

   _____

   _____

   - Matthew 12:36-37

   _____

   _____

   - Proverbs 15:4

   _____

   _____

   - Proverbs 12:18

   _____

   _____

   - Proverbs 18:21

   _____

   _____

SCRIPTURE MEDITATION

For he that will love life, and see good days, let him refrain his tongue from evil, and his lips that they speak no guile (1 Peter 3:10 AKJV).

WISDOM FROM THE RICK-TION-ARY

"Stop beating yourself up and start building yourself up." (1/23/07)

PRAYER

Lord, help me to understand that my words have consequences in the natural and the spiritual realm. Help me to meditate on Your Word and spend time with You because "out of the abundance of the heart the mouth speaketh" (Matthew 12:34 AKJV). Help me to be aware of my thoughts. Help me to catch negative words before I speak them. Let me see my situation from Your perspective and not my limited view. Let my words be filled with the Sprit and life so I can also be an encouragement to others with the words I speak.

VIDEO LINK

www.RICKIERUSH.com/ThePendulum-Ch10

ENDNOTES

1. Jancee Dunn, "Negative Self-Talk: 9 Ways to Silence Your Inner Critic," *The Huffington Post*, April 6, 2013, http://www .huffingtonpost.com/2013/04/06/negative-self-talk-think -positive_n_3009832.html(accessed 8/14/14).

2. "Michael Jordan," BrainyQuote, http://www.brainyquote.com/ quotes/quotes/m/michaeljor127660.html (accessed 8/14/14).

3. Margaret Moore, "How Do You Spot Negative Self-Talk?" *Psychology Today,* August 23, 2009, http://www .psychologytoday.com/blog/life-changes/200908/how-do-you -spot-negative-self-talk (accessed 8/14/14).

4. Elizabeth Scott, "Reduce Stress and Improve Your Life with Positive Self Talk," *About.com;* http://stress.about.com/od/ optimismspirituality/a/positiveselftak.htm (accessed 8/14/14).

Chapter 11

IT'S TIME TO COME BACK SWINGING!

I know the enemy is probably trying to convince you that you are defeated. Just remember: satan is a liar, and he is working overtime because he knows you are so close to victory. Your blessing is right here, in the midst of your difficult times, so prepare to receive it.

Do you remember Jesus' purpose for coming to earth? He came to destroy the works of the enemy (see 1 John 3:8). In fact, Jesus spent so much of His earthly ministry healing people that He is known as the Great Physician. The Bible records many people Jesus healed as He walked the earth.[1] You can rejoice in knowing that He is still the Great Physician performing those same healing miracles today. *It is your time!* So, at this *exact* moment, know that you are not alone in your difficulties; Jesus is and has been with you all along, and He wants to use His power to heal you.

Once when I was speaking of the ways to speed our healing, one of the teenagers in our church said, "So, reading the Bible and praying every day is like taking those chewable vitamins our parents used to give us?" I thought, *He's right.* Like vitamins, the "prescriptions" in this chapter help us stay healthy and energized, help us fight germs, sicknesses and diseases, and provide nutritious tips we need to grow and develop properly. So, using his analogy, consider these prescriptions for ensuring your victory.

THE GREAT PHYSICIAN'S PRESCRIPTIONS FOR YOUR VICTORY

1. Seek God's Word

2. Get under an anointed ministry

3. Have faith

4. Pray

5. Praise and worship

6. Know your authority

7. Take every thought captive

8. Have a heart of gratitude

9. Connect heart to heart with the Lord

Before we get started, I just want to encourage you that these disciplines should be applied for a lifetime. When people tell me, "I read the Bible and it didn't work for me," I always ask, "How regularly and how long?" Our lives are a marathon, not a sprint, and we must set our pace with that in mind.

PRESCRIPTION #1: SEEK GOD'S WORD

God's Word will heal you. That's a bold, but true statement. Psalm 107:20 tells us, *"He sent out his word and healed them; he rescued them from the grave."* God's Word is medicine, and the moment you start reading it, praying it, speaking it out loud, meditating on it, and believing it, doses of God's healing power start to flow throughout your heart, mind, and soul.

Step 1: Get your daily dose of nutrients; read God's Word every day.

Reading and studying God's Word regularly nurtures and protects our spiritual, physical, and emotional health. When I didn't continuously fill my spirit with God's Word, I would find myself losing energy and getting weak and deflated, which made it much easier for the enemy to discourage me. So, access your healing by filling yourself with God's Word on a regular basis.

Reading the Word is a discipline. If you don't make an effort, it won't just happen. Just like we must eat to feed our natural bodies, we must discipline ourselves to feed our spirit. Make it a habit. Put your Bible where you'll see it, in the bathroom or your nightstand.

Reading several verses or a chapter is a great way to start your day. Everybody's appetite is different; read until you feel full. Most people like and can relate to the wisdom found in Proverbs, and there are 31 chapters. You can read one for each day of the month.

Another helpful tip is to make sure you get a version of the Bible that's easy to read. You'll enjoy it more if you aren't tripping over "thees" and "thous" and "wherefores." (By the way, I nicknamed my bed "the Word." That way I impress people with my spirituality when I tell them, "I just spent seven hours in the Word.")

Step 2: Meditate on His Word.

As a young pastor, I learned that I had to feed myself daily by meditating on the Word of God. Doing this keeps us filled up with God's Spirit and power. Psalm 1:2 (AKJV) instructs, *"But his delight is in the law of the Lord; and in his law doth he meditate day and night."* Meditating means to speak the Word to yourself and to speak to yourself about the Word. The Hebrew word for "meditation" actually means to speak or to mutter and in order to know Him, you must speak to yourself about Him, think about or ponder on Him.

Meditation is a faith builder. Speak to yourself about God's promises. David understood this. He meditated on who God was to him, and when he stood before Goliath, his faith was strong and his fear was weak.

God's Word is a treasure. We reap its benefits if we think of it throughout the day under the influence of the Holy Spirit's revelation. *"I will meditate on your precepts and fix my eyes on your ways"* (Psalm 119:15 ESV). Pick your favorite verse and try fixing your eyes on it today.

Step 3: Take special vitamins when needed.

Just as vitamins provide nutrients for specific parts of our bodies, God has provided a specific Word for your specific situation. Let's take a quick inventory of what's in God's medicine chest.

What is God's medicine for those of us who engage in negative self-talk that the world promotes? His medicine is Romans 12:2, *"Don't become so well-adjusted to your culture that you fit into it without even thinking. Instead, fix your attention on God. You'll be changed from the inside out..."* (MSG).

Does God have a prescription for those who have been hurt by family members or close friends? Of course. Get an entire tablespoon of Ephesians 6:12 (AKJV) and refill as needed:

> *For we wrestle not against flesh and blood, but against principalities, against powers, against the rulers of the darkness of this world, against spiritual wickedness in high places.*

God has already prescribed your solution; it's in His Word. Memorize those specific Bible verses or stories that speak to your situation. That way, when you feel yourself starting to deflate, you can take God's medicine and seal the puncture wound quickly. Consider the following biblical prescriptions.

Step 3: Declare the Word over your life and circumstances.

Declaring the Word over your life and circumstances is another prescription that destroys the enemy. We know that the Word is true and cannot be changed. The Lord said, *"I am watching over my word to perform it"* (Jeremiah 1:12 ESV), so start declaring it. I'm not talking about "I need a Lamborghini." Take the verses you just found about your situation and agree by declaring them aloud.

David spoke and sang declarations of encouragement, then he wrote them down, and that's how we got the book of Psalms. Speaking or singing God's declarations over your life is powerful. For instance, Psalm 91 gives us clear insight on the protection He provides for those who abide in Him. It's a great place to start. No evil will befall me. No plague will come near my house (see Psalm 91:10).

Here are a few more to get you started. Declare these out loud:

- I am more than a conqueror (Romans 8:37).

- I am fearfully and wonderfully made (Psalm 139:14).

- You will never leave me or forsake me (Hebrews 13:5).

- I can do all things because You strengthen me (Philippians 4:13).

- The gates of hell will not prevail against me (Matthew 16:18).

Step 4: Devotionally pray the Word.

Devotionally praying the Word is a combination of prayer and declaration. Sit before the Lord with an open Bible and with an open heart. Paraphrase the Scripture as a prayer back to Him. At the same time you're also declaring it to your spirit. Here's an example of how I do this with Psalm 1:1-3:

> *Blessed is the one who does not walk in step with the wicked or stand in the way that sinners take or sit in the company of mockers, but whose delight is in the law of the Lord, and who meditates on his law day and night. That person is like a tree planted by streams of water, which yields its fruit in season and whose leaf does not wither—whatever that person does prospers.*

As I read this verse I pray it to the Lord like this.

Lord, I thank You that I am blessed. Help me to make godly choices by avoiding the influence of the wicked, the sinners, and the mockers. Help me to delight in Your Word and to meditate on it always. I thank You that I'm becoming like a strong tree planted by the stream. Lord, I know You will help me produce lasting fruit and keep my leaves from withering. Thank You that whatever I do prospers.

If you read God's Word daily, ingesting those verses and stories that speak healing specifically to your situation, declare and pray them, you will start to feel better. Your energy and your appetite will return. Feast on God's Word, consume His medicine, and walk in your healing! As the Scripture notes, *"You're blessed when you've worked up a good appetite for God. He's food and drink in the best meal you'll ever eat"* (Matthew 5:6 MSG).

PRESCRIPTION #2: GET UNDER THE COVERING OF AN ANOINTED MINISTRY

If you want quality health care, you must seek out top quality insurance. Likewise, if you are going to heal and grow spiritually, you need to get under the covering of an anointed ministry.

You need to be an active member of an anointed church. The Bible tells us in Hebrews 10:25 not to forsake the gathering of ourselves together. Church is where you need to be if you're coming out of depression. Being isolated puts you right where satan wants you. You need the support and testimonies of your family that Jesus already paid the insurance premium!

Beyond that, you need a pastor who has been called by God, to explain every detail of the coverage policy (Bible) to you, so you understand all the benefits to which you're entitled!

Signs of an anointed ministry include: 1) God's Word is being accurately taught, 2) God speaks directly to you through the pastor, and 3) you *see* God's harvest through growth in the ministry—both spiritually and materially.

PRESCRIPTION #3: FAITH

My daughter Kristian called me once when she was driving through a low-lying roadway after a heavy rainfall. I could hear the panic in her voice when I picked up the phone.

"Dad, the water is rising. I don't know what to do!"

I told her, "Kristian, keep pressing on the gas...stay on the gas."

Exasperated, she replied, "Dad, if I stay on the gas, I'm going to hit the car in front of me!"

"Steer around him, but, no matter what, stay on the gas. If you don't, the water will consume your engine, you'll lose control and get swept away. Trust me, Kris, just stay on the gas."

Kris shouted, "OH NO, DAD, I THINK I'M DRIVING DOWN THE MEDIAN!"

"Kris, that's okay. As long as you're still moving forward. You just keep your foot on the accelerator. Stay on the gas!" I heard her sniffing. Kristian was crying because she was focused on the turbulent waters swirling around her. "Kristian, stop worrying about what you see. Concentrate on my voice. I'll get you through this. I promise. I've done this before."

"I'm so scared!"

"I know you can't see your way through it, but focus on my voice. I know exactly what I'm doing! Cry if you need to, but stay on the gas."

After a few more yards and a few more sniffles, Kris exclaimed, "Dad, I think I'm headed up a hill. I can't see it yet, but I'm pressing the accelerator, and I've got traction." And just like that, she was on her way again.

This incident got me thinking how all the devil needs to seep in and take over is just a little doubt. Satan will use that to pry open a crack that will flood your vehicle, and instead of you driving through the water, the water will drive you wherever it pleases.

Just like I told Kris to focus on my voice instead of the torrential waters she was actually seeing, God calls us to have faith and trust Him. Ask yourself: Am I so focused on my difficult situation that my faith is shrinking? Don't let the turbulent, boisterous winds of your situation cause you to miss God's instructions. This is precisely the moment when you must apply your faith.

Apply Your Faith

Noah is a great example of applied faith. God asked him to build an ark in the middle of the desert. Also keep in mind that it had never rained before. Not one drop. Yet Noah began building in faith. The ark was huge. It took 120 years to build. No wonder Noah was the first person in the Bible who was called righteous. Do you have an ark you're hesitating to build? Faith that pleases God is faith in action.

Most likely you have heard James 2:17, that "faith without works is dead," but I like The Message translation, which states, *"Isn't it obvious that God-talk without God-acts is outrageous nonsense?"* Faith needs to be acted upon or it's not really faith. Applying your faith can be as easy as agreeing with Him. Shout a resounding *Amen* to what He asks of you, which means *Yes, I agree.*

If you really believe the Bible is God's Word and believe He's who He said He is and that He'll do what He said He would do, how would your life be different? How would it affect the risks you take? The way you spend your money? These are the actions that we need to take to apply our faith. Take Him at His Word. Row away from the shore and jump out of the boat. Attempt something that's so big that if it's not God, you'll surely fail.

Strengthen Your Faith

There are three ways to strengthen your faith: 1) read the Word, 2) learn to speak faith, and 3) encourage others.

God knows that if we are reading His Word regularly, memorizing it, and applying it to our lives, we are increasing our capacity to *speak faith.* Satan uses difficult times, problems, and situations to get us *stuck* and to scare us so much that we won't take a swing at him.

The good news is God only requires us to have mustard seed-size faith (see Matthew 17:20). He is so powerful that He can take that tiny amount of faith and steer us safely out of the low-lying flooded areas. So, no matter what bad reports you received, you must continue to tap into your faith and say, "I'm still all right!" Consider your obstacles as merely stepping stones, paving your path to victory. You will have to work muscles you never even knew you had, but in the end, your faith will be stronger.

When we speak faith to others at church, we are, in fact, ministering to ourselves as well. By recounting the many healing miracles that Jesus performed, by whispering encouraging verses to ourselves and to others, we strengthen our faith and theirs. I was able to help my daughter Kristian because I had been through a similar situation. Even when her faith waned, I had enough faith to carry us both. So, as I told her and many others, "Keep pressing. Stay on the gas, and you'll come through!"

PRESCRIPTION #4: PRAYER

Praying allows you to give your problems to Him. He tells you specifically to cast your burdens on Him (see 1 Peter 5:7), and prayer is just the prescription to do that.

A Life-Changing Revelation

We all have areas of weakness that we go to great pains to hide. We carry these unnecessary loads because we fear disappointing people and damaging our relationships.

> When your life is turned upside down, God is ready to turn it back around.

Satan was taking great delight whispering in my ear that my selfish desires killed my mother. I believed I was guilty because I couldn't rescue her. For years I was afraid to talk to God because I believed He was just another name on the list of people who were disappointed in me. I pictured Him shaking His head and sighing loudly or maybe grabbing a lightning bolt to hurl in my direction. So I naturally kept my distance. But when I found out that God was a loving Father whom I couldn't disappoint, I found freedom. I got honest with Him. I told Him everything! That's when He could start cleaning me up. And to my great relief—no lightning bolts.

Here's what I learned: God chose me to be His son knowing every sin I'd ever commit—every lie, deceptive thought, every evil intention. He knew it all before He chose me. Disappointment only happens when you have unfulfilled expectations, so how could He be disappointed with me? He didn't have expectations that other people put on me or I put on myself. My failures were no surprise to Him.

God is not appalled at your weaknesses, sins, and failures.

Your worst mistakes can be the greatest way He can prove His grace and mercy to you. When you are overcome with shame and self-hatred, don't run *from* Jesus like I did, run *to* Him in prayer! He's the only One who can help you get free.

I want you to experience the same freedom that I found in prayer so I've listed several keys. Remember, you simply cannot disappoint God, so go to Him with everything! You'll be surprised how simple and satisfying prayer really is.

Real, sincere, heartfelt prayer is done in private.

What we think of as "formal prayer," praying out loud, praying in public is important, but this ongoing internal dialogue between you and your God is most important. When you talk to Him you're talking about issues of your heart that you can't tell others.

Be yourself.

Don't try to pray long, complicated prayers. Don't try to impress. Keep it simple. It's exactly like talking to your best friend. There is no need to exaggerate or use flowery language. Talk to God much like Kristian talked to me when she was facing those raging waters.

God really wants to hear from you.

We've made prayer too formal and too complicated. It's really just an ongoing minute-by-minute talk with God, all day long. Now before you get too intimidated by that definition, let me explain the different components for you. Remember in the self-talk chapter we established that there are thoughts going on in your head all the time? And you know that Jesus dwells within you, in your spirit (see 1 Corinthians 6:19). So you merely need to realize several dynamics: 1) you're thinking all day long, and 2) Jesus, living in you, is listening, and 3) you can direct your conversation to Jesus who lives within. So the life of prayer is a constant discussion with the One who loves you deeply.

God made you to talk to Him, and He longs to hear your voice.

Prayer says, "I know I don't have it all together."

Right about now you might be panicking when you really realize that Jesus is hearing all your thoughts. But, He's known them all along and He loves you anyway. Jeremiah 17:9 states, *"The heart is deceitful above all things and beyond cure. Who can understand it?"* The answer to Jeremiah's question is—Jesus understands it. *"For he knows our frame; he remembers that we are dust"* (Psalm 103:14 ESV). Remember my life-changing discovery? It's impossible to disappoint Him. Fortunately we have the ability to confess these negative thoughts and we know Jesus promises to always forgive (see 1 John 1:9). He's there within you and He's *for* you in your weakness.

"Therefore, there is now no condemnation for those who are in Christ Jesus" (Romans 8:1). His cross has delivered you from shame and death. The question is not: Is Jesus disgusted with or mad at me? The question is: Do you want to hold on to those thoughts? Jesus, your Friend, will be happy to take them from you. It isn't a fast process, but if you give them to Him—"Lord, I don't like this thought; will You take it?"—eventually they will evaporate and be replaced.

Prayer involves expressing your pain, articulating your desire, and describing your need.

As you spend more time with Him your friendship will deepen. Just imagine, you live life with your Best Friend all the time. And just like you want to share everything with your earthly best friend, you'll want to share your pain, desires, and needs with your internal Best Friend. And the really amazing thing is this Best Friend happens to be your God and your Creator. There's nothing you can't tell Him because He already knows it. Get honest with your deepest fears, needs, insecurities, and desires.

God always knows what we're trying to say, even when we don't have the words.

Sometimes really good friends don't even have to talk. Every time discouragement causes you to sigh, that's prayer. Every time you weep, that's prayer. *"You keep track of all my sorrows. You have collected all my tears in your bottle. You have recorded each one in your book"* (Psalm 56:8 NLT). He knows us when we're strong and when we're weak, and He's for us, not against us.

Prayer is a two-way conversation.

Now there's a second part to prayer. If you're the only one who's talking, it's called a monologue—a good friendship requires both taking and listening, a dialogue. With practice comes the ability to hear His voice. Give Him your complete attention. Jesus is about to talk to you and what He says about you is the most important thing in your world.

Hebrews 7:25 tells us that He lives to make intercession for believers. As we draw closer to our Friend, He shares the burdens on His heart. When this happens we find ourselves praying for what God is concerned about. Prayer is both pouring out your heart before your Friend and listening to His heart poured out before you.

You need a God-ordained agenda, and you get it by talking to Him.

Listen for His encouragement because He can identify with your pain. *"Even though Jesus was God's Son, he learned obedience from the things he suffered"* (Hebrews 5:8 NLT). He is known as a man of sorrows, despised, rejected and acquainted with deepest grief (see Isaiah 53:3). Rest in the knowledge that as you pour out your heart to Him, He understands your pain and suffering. He can help you get over the next seemingly insurmountable hurdle. He gives us wisdom and strategies to get free of our discouragement.

So we pour out our emotions, we pour out our questions, our pain and requests before our Friend. And we listen for His answers and the burdens on His heart. And that, my friend is prayer.

PRESCRIPTION #5: DEFEATING THE ENEMY THROUGH WORSHIP AND PRAISE

Any time you're feeling deflated, pull out this next powerful prescription. The enemy hates it when we worship and praise God because God inhabits the praises of His people (see Psalm 22:3).

Most people think that praise and worship are the same, but there's a difference. Praise is a thank you for what He's done. Worship is deeper. We honor Him for who He is, whether we've received the answer to our prayer or not.

You'll frequently hear "Let's stand and worship the Lord by lifting our voices." But worship is more personal than that, it's private. Just you and your God. Set aside intentional time to come to Him with no pretenses, but with boldness and assurance that He's going to receive your worship with great joy.

The posture of worship is varied. What does it look like? It looks like doing something that you believe He will accept. You can prostrate yourself before Him. The Bible speaks of bowing down at His feet in submission. You may want to find a place where you can kneel. Find what works for you. It doesn't matter what it looks like to anyone else as long He receives your worship.

Work as Worship

I've heard the story that during the Renaissance a huge cathedral was being built. Someone dropped by to watch and began talking to the various artisans. "What are you doing?" he asked a stone mason. "I'm building this wall straight and true." "What are you doing?" he asked another. "I'm building stained glass windows," was the reply. He walked to the back where an elderly woman was pushing a broom. "What are you doing?" he inquired. Her face lit up and she replied, "I'm building a cathedral to the glory of God."

Did you know that your work is also an act of worship? The same Hebrew word means both worship and work.[2] *"And whatever you do, whether in word or deed, do it all in the name of the Lord Jesus..."* (Colossians 3:17). You don't have to be a worship leader to worship the Lord at your job. Martin Luther said, "A dairy maid can milk cows to the glory of God."[3]

Turn your labors into worship by doing them as unto the Lord. That way, everything is an act of worship. Whether you're in the boardroom or the laundry room, it doesn't matter. At work your main focus is to do a good job for Him. Pleasing your boss is a bonus. When working as unto the Lord becomes a lifestyle, then your daily efforts are transported to the heavens as worship and you *"let your light shine before others, that they may see your good deeds and glorify your Father in heaven"* (Matthew 5:16).

Praise

I'm the choir leader at my church and I love to sing praises. Sing declarations throughout the day because you love Him, or sing in the spirit and *"make music from your heart to the Lord"* (Ephesians 5:19). As you go through the day, feed your spirit with anything from classic hymns to contemporary worship songs.

If you listen to music that is neutral, you won't experience spiritual growth. If you listen to something that plants thoughts in your mind that aren't godly, you're going to lose ground. You can't unlisten to something once it's in your brain. Be careful what you allow inside.

Here's a great way you can use praise to defeat the enemy. When he whispers in your ear, capture his thoughts, renounce them, and praise God for the opposite. For example, if you hear, "You're a failure, just quit," then you can confidently say, *"I am not a failure. I can do all things through Christ who strengthens me"* (Philippians 4:13 NKJV). If you use the enemy's voice as a reminder to praise God, it shuts him up and sends him packing.

PRESCRIPTION #6: THE BELIEVER'S AUTHORITY (HOW TO THROW SATAN OUT OF YOUR HOUSE)

We can no longer allow satan to dictate our feelings or our actions. He has no right in our lives. Rise up and overcome him using this powerful prescription—the authority God has given you.

My Grandson's Stick

I love animals and have quite the menagerie at my home. Fish, dogs, birds, swans, geese, horses, cats—you name it. I have a stick that I've used to train them. Of course my grandson, Kaiden, wanted a stick also to make him look like Grandpa. As we walked, none of the animals paid any attention to his stick. Then I got an idea. I handed Kaiden *my* stick. It was taller than he was and he had trouble wielding it, but when he finally held it out, he was quite amused to see the animals, which just minutes ago were ignoring him, suddenly lay down in submission or roll over. He had no power or innate strength over them, some of which outweighed him, but I imparted my authority and power to him and the animals respected it. I smiled toward the sky and thought, *Okay, God, point taken.*

He's Given Us Power Tools

The Bible is full of Scriptures on God's authority imparted to Christians. According to Luke 10:19 Jesus has given us authority to trample on snakes and scorpions and to overcome *all* the power of the enemy; nothing will harm us. Satan has a measure of power, but we've been given power over his power.

Paul prayed that Christians would know *"the exceeding greatness of his power to* [those] *who believe..."* (Ephesians 1:19 AKJV). He continues:

> *That power is the same as the mighty strength he exerted when he raised Christ from the dead and seated him at his right hand in the heavenly realms, far above all rule and authority, power and dominion, and every name that is invoked, not only in the present age but also in the one to come* (Ephesians 1:19-21).

He has given this authority to you, the same power that God used to raise Jesus from the dead, so you can stand against satan. James 4:7 says, *"Resist the devil, and he will flee from you,"* and Ephesians 6:10 exhorts us to *"be strong in the Lord and in his mighty power."*

Paul describes the full armor of God that we must put on to fight satan. But notice that it's a command. *You* must put on each piece. God won't put the armor on you.

> *Put on the full armor of God, so that you can take your stand against the devil's schemes. ...Stand firm then, with the belt of truth buckled around your waist, with the breastplate of righteousness in place, and with your feet fitted with the readiness that comes from the gospel of peace. In addition to all this, take up the shield of faith, with which you can extinguish all the flaming arrows of the evil one. Take the helmet of salvation and the sword of the Spirit, which is the word of God* (Ephesians 6:11,14-17).

His armor and weapons are all available to you. God is there to back you up with His Word, but you have to use the authority He has provided. Don't pray and ask God to fight satan for you. You have received the power and the authority to take the Word of God, the name of Jesus, and the power of the Holy Spirit to run satan and his luggage out of every area of your life declaring, "IN THE NAME OF JESUS, GET OUT AND STAY OUT!"

PRESCRIPTION #7: TAKE EVERY THOUGHT CAPTIVE

After putting on the full armor each morning to resist the enemy's fiery darts, then you must take every thought captive (see 2 Corinthians 10:5). The following information is paraphrased from the novel *The Designer Bag at the Garbage Dump* written by my friend, Jackie Macgirvin. Taking every thought captive is hand-to-hand combat with the enemy, but it's well worth the cost. It leads to truth and peace instead of stress and anxiety. God doesn't have stress, He laughs uproariously in the face of His enemies (Psalm 2:4)—and you can too.

Every day you have two choices, you can dwell on and magnify God, or you can dwell on and magnify your problems. If you ruminate on your problems, you give them your worship. You meditate on them like you should be meditating on God's Word. You actually worship the devil when you worry. That's a disturbing thought, but it's true. So let's capture those worship thoughts directed toward satan and send him and them packing.

All day long there is an inner dialogue raging in your mind. When a worrisome thought pops in, ask yourself, "Where did that come from? God, yourself, or the devil?" The devil *"is a liar and the father of lies"* (John 8:44). Train your mind to reject his lies because whoever controls your mind controls you. Don't let his negative thoughts go unchallenged or they will take root and you will believe them as truth.

Visualize yourself marking the cross over the lie and saying out loud, "I resist and rebuke this lie in Jesus' name and I replace it with the truth of...." Then quote a related Scripture. This is how you take every thought captive.

> You have two choices, dwell on and magnify God, or dwell on and magnify your problems.

When Peter allowed his mind to lie to him about the wind and the waves, he was sunk—literally. Be careful with your negative thoughts. Don't keep them around long enough to let them make a home.

A Good Fight

Paul encourages Timothy to *"Fight the good fight..."* (1 Timothy 6:12). I've engaged in a few elementary school brawls, and I know what a good fight is. A good fight is one you win! The enemy will return again and again. This battle is a marathon, not a sprint. Resist and rebuke the enemy's thoughts and state the truth to yourself, out loud. If you do this, your mind will become a beautiful, peaceful place for you to live.

"The things you take for granted, someone else is praying for."[4]

PRESCRIPTION #8: HAVE A HEART OF GRATITUDE

Trying to break out of discouragement without a heart of gratitude is like trying to drive from Texas to California on a quarter tank of gas. We'll do well for a few miles, but after just a little bit, we wonder why the engine is sputtering. Now we're on the side of the road in the blazing heat.

Gratitude is the ultimate humility. Jesus tells us that *"Apart from me you can do nothing"* (John 15:5). Everything we have is from Him, all the way down to our breath and our beating heart. If today He withdrew either, we would be gone. We can always thank Him for the gift of life.

Psalm 44:8 (NASB) says, *"In God we have boasted all day long, and we will give thanks to Your name forever."* Gratitude moves our focus off our pain and selfish desires. It shifts our focus to the abundant gifts God has lavished on us. The psalmist suggests that gratitude should be a daily habit. Ask yourself, What if I woke up today with only what I thanked God for yesterday? What would I have now?

The enemy works full time to bring us down. It's his job to make us miserable. The ability for us to look past our stresses, trials, and failures to focus on every blessing that remains is an ongoing challenge. It's always been human nature to focus on the negative.

Once again, it's a matter of perspective. I knew a woman in a nursing home who had to start using a walker. She thought it was the end of the world. Then she ended up in a wheelchair. She would watch the people shuffling up and down the hallway with their walkers longing for those days to return.

No matter how bad your situation is, it could always be worse. By God's grace we need to develop the ability to look at our situation and be grateful for whatever good remains. Don't give in to discouragement. Our difficulties are seasons, not indicators that He doesn't love us. The next time you're tempted to say, "God how could You do this to me?" look instead at the cross and say with gratitude, "God, how could you do *this* for me?

Take a few minutes and watch this powerful video on gratitude called My Shoes at http://tinyurl.com/mpgnjyw *or* https://www.youtube.com/watch?v=SolGBZ2f6L0.

PRESCRIPTION #9: CONNECT HEART TO HEART WITH GOD

The enemy's attacks will be much more powerful than they ought to be if we are not making sure this prescription gets filled—spending time in His presence.

I have a personal appointment with God. It's on my schedule every day. I call it white space because nothing is written there. I know the value of meeting Him before I get out of bed. My life is so busy, once my feet touch the floor, every second is eaten up. So the early morning is when He gets my undivided attention and I get His. Even if I oversleep, I don't under-pray. It's a part of my daily routine.

Ask God to make you hungry to be in His presence.

Most people have a daily routine—brushing their teeth, showering, feeding the dog—but they don't have a consistent time to spend with God. Choose a place, choose a time and stick with it. It's costly to spend time with the Lord, it's more costly not to. Pay the price to connect with God and renew your strength (see Isaiah 40:31).

David and Job Look to God's Face

David spent about seven years, from about ages 23-30, living in the wilderness, hiding in caves, fleeing Saul and his army who were trying to kill him (see 1 Samuel 21–27). Many of the psalms he wrote during this time have the theme of being discouraged, cast down, abandoned, etc. He definitely had years when his pendulum was stuck. But David experienced beauty on the ash heap of depression because he knew how to connect with the Lord. Interacting with God was his primary pleasure in life. It sustained him.

When David was discouraged, he turned his eyes away from his negative conditions and looked to the face of God. Psalm 57:7 (AKJV) says, *"My heart is fixed, O God, my heart is fixed...."* When David was running for his life, when he felt the pain of loneliness, he didn't concentrate on his circumstances, he positioned his heart before the Lord.

We become what we look at, we become who we behold.

Job came out the other side of his trial with an intimacy he lacked before. He told God, *"I had heard rumors about You, but now my eyes have seen You"* (Job 42:5).[5] Job experienced God in a new way. He understood that all of his suffering was well worth the experience of having firsthand knowledge of God.

Inside, Not Out There

We won't find our answer "out there" somewhere, we will find our answer from the Lord who dwells inside us, in our spirit. He is our ultimate help. He is our source of comfort during difficult times. He will set us free, fill us up, and cause us to swing back to the other side. Your transformation might not come as fast as you want, but don't give up.

You can't heal your heart, but you can position your heart in front of Him and let Him touch you. This is different from the necessary disciplines of prayer, worship and Bible study.

Here's how you can practically connect with the presence of the Lord. First, seek Him daily. Better to have a little time each day than to shoot for three hours on Saturday and fail. Find a quiet place where you aren't distracted by kids, TV, or the phone. Start with a humble attitude. "God, I can't do anything without You. I need You, reveal Your love for me and give me direction." Get comfortable, close your eyes and take several deep breaths to relax. Picture yourself breathing in the Holy Spirit and breathing out your stress and your anxieties. Invite the Holy Spirit to help you connect with Jesus, who resides inside—in your spirit. You're not looking outside for Him, you're retreating to where He resides—inside—and finding Him there.

Just soak and feel His love. Let Him do what He wants. He might bring up an unresolved issue in need of forgiveness to help clear out the dross. If you don't feel anything, that's okay. Use your faith to stay there. Trust that He's really with you, is smiling over you and enjoying your company. Relax like a child snuggling in the arms of a safe daddy. You don't have to perform, you don't have to prove anything, just be His. Trust that it will be okay and that He loves you. Feel His emotional protection and a sense of well-being. There's not even a need for words.

Over the years I've seen that people who spend significant amounts of time connecting with the Lord in this manner grow strong and mature quickly. The ones who neglect this discipline look pretty much the same year in and year out. In spending time with the Lord, we learn He can change our thoughts, addictions, and heal our wounds in a way that all the good intentions and willpower can't.

Maybe carving out time to spend with God is new to you. Maybe no one ever taught you how, so you've struggled. Jesus was busy while on earth, but He knew the value of connecting with God; He had to leave the crowd and go to that place of being alone with God (see Luke 15:16). That quiet time is a basic ingredient for maturing your relationship with Him. When it comes to intimate times, put God on your schedule. It's like the friend who says, "Let's do lunch." Unless you write it down, it won't happen.

DIFFERENT STROKES FOR DIFFERENT FOLKS

I've tried to give some practical specifics, but all of these prescriptions—prayer, praise, meditation, reading the Word, etc.—are all personal. God isn't boring, so if you're not experiencing success, maybe the technique isn't a proper fit. Use a variety of methods and if it moves in a different direction let it flow.

The same devotional book that you found interesting six months ago might be feeling stale. Put it down and make up your own devotional today. Pray in the Spirit while you take a prayer walk. Find someone who'll pray with you, in person, or make a weekly phone appointment. Download a Bible app and play a game. Infuse the prescriptions into your lifestyle. They are crucial to your victory, but they may look slightly different for you.

Now that I've said that, let me say this: There's a reason these prescriptions are called "disciplines." It takes great discipline to adopt them, and most people never do. Don't give up on your method or technique too soon. It takes about 30 days to form a new habit. I pray you can tell the difference between the tenacious willpower needed to develop a new, powerful spiritual habit, and the frustration of using a method that isn't a good fit for you.

THIS TOO WILL PASS

As you can see there's lots of prescriptions from the Great Physician to help you conquer your depression. I want you to know that even if you're feeling alone and abandoned, you always have help because the Lord is on your side. He is eager and waiting to deliver you. God is good and will always be so. He will never leave or forsake you (see Hebrews 13:5).

Our suffering isn't unique. Everyone in the body of Christ will go through or has gone through times of suffering and depression. They are necessary for our growth. Rejoice during your downtime because God's glory is being revealed to you and in you.

Paul said, *"We rejoice in our sufferings, knowing that suffering produces endurance, and endurance produces character, and character produces hope, and hope does not put us to shame, because God's love has been poured into our hearts through the Holy Spirit who has been given to us"* (Romans 5:3-5 ESV).

We do not glory because we *have* affliction, but in what these afflictions *produce*. God uses these sufferings for exercising, obtaining, and increasing what we need in order to mature—in this case, endurance, character, and hope. Above all, we have God's love poured upon us and we have been given the Holy Spirit, the Comforter who will teach us all things (see John 14:26). What more do we need in order to overcome in our season of discouragement? Nothing more than God the Father, God the Son, and God the Holy Spirit.

WHAT I REALLY WANT YOU TO REMEMBER

Jesus said that He came to earth to destroy the works of the devil. He's still doing that today. We can speed our healing by following the Great Physician's prescriptions for victory:

- Seek God's Word

- Get under an anointed ministry

- Have faith

- Pray

- Praise and worship

- Know your authority

- Take every thought captive

- Have a heart of gratitude

- Connect heart to heart with the Lord

APPLICATION EXERCISE

1. Pick one prescription off the list that you'll commit to do for a lifetime.

_____

2. Write a realistic plan to implement it. How? When? Where? Be very specific.

_____

_____

_____

_____

3. Get your calendar and schedule it.

_____

_____

4. Write down any resources you might need: a different Bible version, a study guide, a gratitude journal, a worship CD, etc.

_____

_____

5. Put this book down and do your first session.

_____

_____

SCRIPTURE MEDITATION

The Son of God appeared for this purpose, to destroy the works of the devil (1 John 3:8 NASB).

WISDOM FROM THE RICK-TION-ARY

"The deeper we go in God, the higher we
go in victorious living." (6/11/09)

PRAYER

Lord, I know that there are things I've ignored that I should have been doing and I ask You to forgive me. I ask for Your grace, which I will need to stick with the plan I've made. Help me to remember when I encounter a few bumps in the road to forgive myself and start again. Lord, I need more of You. Please help me to find You as my Healer through this new prescription.

VIDEO LINK

www.RICKIERUSH.com/ThePendulum-Ch11

ENDNOTES

1. John 4:46, 5:2, 9:1, 11:11; Mark 1:21,29, 4:24, 8:22; Matt. 8:1,5,14, 9:1,20,27,32, 12:22, 17:14, 20:29; Luke 4:31, 6:6, 7:11, 8:26, 13:10, 14:1, 17:11, 22:50. Ben, "A list of Jesus' Healings," Christian Healing Today, posted October 16, 2008, http://christianhealingtoday.com/2008/10/16/a-list-of-jesus-healings/#sthash.clWmUTbX.dpuf (accessed 8/14/14).

2. William D. Bjoraker, "Word Study: (AVODAH)—Work/Worship," The General Council of the Assemblies of God, http://ag.org/top/church_workers/wrshp_gen_avodah.cfm (accessed 8/15/14).

3. *The Westminster Collection of Christian Quotations*, compiled by Martin H. Manser (Louisville, KY: Westminister John Knox Press, 2001), 403.

4. J. Johnson, "The Things You Take for Granted Someone Else is Praying For," Searchquotes, http://www.searchquotes.com/viewimage/The_Things_You_Take_For_Granted_Someone_Else_Is_Praying_For/732/ (accessed 8/15/14).

5. *Holman Christian Standard Bible*; copyright © 1999, 2000, 2002, 2003, 2009 by Holman Bible Publishers, Nashville, Tennessee. All rights reserved.

Chapter 12

IT'S TIME TO SET THE RECORD STRAIGHT

The Bible speaks in Malachi 3:16 about a book of remembrance. That's what this book is for me. As I was writing I remembered how things went down in my life. I remembered how all satan's baggage came in. How I lived hurt and how upset, but I kept on living. Sometimes I got up bruised. But as I've lived the different chapters, I'm pleased to share how the story ends.

The more the enemy tries to fight us, the stronger the anointing becomes upon us.

I was born on March 9, 1964, on the third floor of Parkland Hospital. My mother told me that when she found out she was pregnant with me, she just cried and cried and cried. Her labor with me was hard because of what she was about to deliver. It's different when you raise a king. I was called to preach.

Satan knew it, too. The only way for me not to preach was for him to take me out as a boy. And the only way to take someone out is to destroy the person before his destiny arrives.

Being only ten when my mom passed away, the enemy probably would have gotten me had not my mom, my grandma, and my grandpa covered me with so much prayer. They brought me up in the way of the Lord and taught me to worship Him with all my might.

Since satan knows that faith comes by hearing (see Romans 10:17), he'll do whatever he can to cause us to believe lies. In addition to using that preacher at Mama's funeral to convince me that I should be angry at God, satan planted inside me the thought that men were evil. I hated teenage boys. This started early and developed into a 100 percent hatred for anything male.

I was called to preach.

That year in fourth grade, I wasn't functioning well. My mom, who was my greatest cheerleader in life, was now gone. I went to live with my adopted parents and their three children. I had all-consuming guilt and anger. And I feared the guys who killed my mama would come back and kill me. I wasn't going to go to school, listen, or even grow up.

I became the bad student no one liked. My attitude was, "Whip me; I don't care." The last straw was when I set the lawn on fire at school. So to keep me from disturbing the rest of the kids, they moved me to the Special Education class with no explanation. I didn't know what it was. I just knew it was where the kids who were losers went. It became really hard to shake that label.

I started crying out at night in my dreams. My stepbrothers told my stepmom, and they thought I was losing it, hallucinating, having terrible nightmares. One night my stepmom came in to wake me, but when she listened, I wasn't having bad dreams, I was preaching about Moses. She took me to a preacher, and he told me, "Talk to the church. Say what you said in your dreams." I said, "Go down, Moses, tell Pharaoh to let my people go." That was the beginning of my preaching.

I was just a kid giving speeches at church and still missing Mom.

Although I wasn't doing well in school, I was doing well at church. Before I knew it I was being sent everywhere to speak. I didn't know I was a preacher. I was just a kid giving speeches at church and still missing Mom. That's how I became the boy preacher.

My stepparents made me study and practice. I had to learn Bible terms. Heaven forbid if I mispronounced *Pharaoh*. It was a bunch of work and no fun. In a month I preached about 8-10 times. I never got my childhood back.

My stepparents were raising a giant who thought he was always going to be a midget. I was very short in high school. It was embarrassing to have a girlfriend who could pick me up. The girls kept calling me "little brother." I'd say, "I don't want to be your brother, I want to be your man."

Football wasn't any better. When I tried to run onto the field my coach would yell, "Rush, get your tail back." If someone asked me what position I played, I'd say, "tail back." (A few decades later my coach showed up at church and I asked why he never played me. He said, "Because we wanted to win.")

For years, the enemy has been helping God get a bad rap for things He never did or that weren't part of His perfect plan. Satan was after me and my gift to preach the gospel to the poor. Guess who didn't talk to God anymore after hearing that He needed a "rose" for His garden? Guess who wouldn't pray for mothers who were sick after his mom died? I wouldn't do it because I was disappointed with God.

> I found out really fast that leadership means your flaws will get exposed.

Probably the same people who brought you the myth that big boys don't cry are responsible for the belief that people who have been called by God don't have issues. I had to carry God's Word while dealing with the natural trials of life that come to a boy growing into a man—all in the public eye.

I found out really fast that leadership means your flaws will get exposed.

Everyone has something wrong with them when God calls. He has never called a saint to do anything. People *become* saints. None of the disciples were even saved. David was an adulterer, Paul was a murderer, etc. Everyone He calls He qualifies. Much later in life I learned it was okay to bite off more than I could chew; because even if it was too much for me, I knew it wasn't too much for Him.

When I was 18, I began to understand Jesus' words in John 10:10, that there is a thief who came to steal my joy, kill me, and ultimately destroy my destiny. But God had better things in store for me—to give me life, to give me a future, and to fulfill my purpose.

Satan uses our past disappointments with the Lord as an opportunity to tell us that we can't depend on Him. We may think, *He already took away something dear to me in the past, why would I trust Him now?* When I was growing up, if people couldn't explain a tragedy, they would say, "God's too wise to make a mistake." It sounded creepy to say that the devil came and stole someone's baby. So if there was no good way to explain it, they just said it was God, which turned people sour toward Him. Who do they pray to for help if God is the one afflicting them? How do they ask God for healing if they think He gave them cancer?

SETTING THE RECORD STRAIGHT

As I said earlier, my search for answers led me to the book of Job. God confirmed to me, saying, "I was not the One who took her, but I have her." I want to share this with you so you never wound people by telling them that God took away something they dearly loved.

We have 70-80 appointed years to live on this earth. Sometimes we don't take care of ourselves, sometimes our bodies just wear out. Sometimes other people's actions affect us. Death will always come for us and those we love, but we cannot allow that event to break our relationship with God. Satan has robbed far too many people because of this teaching.

I've heard more than my fair share of teenagers dying in horrific ways, people falling asleep at the wheel, and drive-by shootings. I can stand up at funerals and tell the truth now, with confidence and conviction, that God didn't give a child cancer; He didn't send a father to drown his babies; He didn't send a young man to gun down your son in the street. God is too big to make a mistake—it was not planned like that.

GOD *ALLOWS* TRIALS FOR OUR GROWTH...

Though God wasn't the one who stole from Job, satan couldn't have taken anything away unless God allowed him to do so. God allows trials to come to us for three reasons:

1. To mature us so we can handle the blessings He desires to send to us;

2. To deepen our relationship with Him; and

3. To make us more Christlike.

...To Mature Us

God knew what He had in store for Job, and Job couldn't have received it unless he experienced loss. God wanted to bless him more than he could ask or ever imagine (see Ephesians 3:20). Unfortunately, prosperity usually ruins us, so God *protects* us with problems.

Many things happen when we prosper: more anointing, more favor, more money, more ease, and many times these options cause us to give in to temptations we didn't have before. If we're not prepared in advance for the day of blessing, it can ruin us. Life is full of stories of those who experienced instant success—lotto winners, entertainers, and star athletes—who end up years later broke, drug addicted, or dead.

...To Deepen Our Relationship

God also allows trials to deepen our relationship with Him. We sometimes feel, "Because I know and love God, He's not going to allow me to go through suffering." God's plan is too big for us to have such a shallow relationship with Him. He wants to take us deeper. Unfortunately, it's human nature to be apathetic toward God until we encounter problems. As He walks us through this season, we develop a testimony of deliverance so that we know God is real and it causes our relationship with Him to go deeper.

Are you mature enough that He can trust you with a blessing?

God could have prevented all of the suffering and pain Job experienced. But if He had done so, Job would have been pleased to live his life just enjoying his current relationship with God—and God wanted more for Job.

The apostle Paul brings perspective to what he lost and what he willingly gave up in order to gain Christ:

> *At one time all these things were important to me. But because of Christ, I decided that they are worth nothing. Not only these things, but now I think that all things are worth nothing compared with the greatness*

of knowing Christ Jesus my Lord. Because of Christ, I lost all these things, and now I know that they are all worthless trash. All I want now is Christ (Philippians 3:7-8 Easy-to-Read Version).

Paul not only counted these losses and sacrifices as less valuable than his relationship with Christ, they would have weakened or even ruined him. He counted them as "worthless trash" when they competed with the value of knowing Christ.

...To Make Us More Christlike

God is aware of and watching every trial. *Sometimes He allows in His mercy what He could have prevented by His power.* Whether we like it or not, He gives us His grace and prepares us to go through depressing and sometimes tragic experiences so that we come out more refined and more Christlike. Our earthly goal is to be conformed to the image of God's Son (Romans 8:29). *God has a bigger purpose than just our happiness.*

His mercy sometimes comes disguised as a significant trial.

We are willing soldiers who signed up for God's army, ready and prepared for battle. He sees our efforts and knows when we are being attacked. He is not surprised at our suffering and actually allows the enemy to attack us, helping us grow for His glory. As painful as this is, it only serves to make us stronger.

God's anointing is His supernatural power inside of us in the midst of our suffering. When our trials become too overwhelming,

Christ's power is made strong within us and His grace is sufficient to sustain us. *"But he said to me, 'My grace is sufficient for you...'"* (2 Corinthians 12:9). God's grace must empower us to grow through what we cannot endure on our own. *We frequently misunderstand this when we're in the middle of the fire and are unable to find Him. But He is there and His help and compassion are real—and you will eventually see His deliverance.*

20/20 HINDSIGHT

With more than 40 years of hindsight, I can look back and see what was the enemy and what was the Lord. As for all the disappointments and trials, they were seasons I had to *get to* in order to *go through* and *grow through*. But they could not keep me from my destiny.

And you will *go through* and *grow through* your discouraging times, too. But maybe right now you feel a little like Jonah, burned out, discouraged, and possibly even on the run. Can't you just picture him in those confined, dark quarters of his water taxi, sloshing back and forth? Seaweed wrapped around his head, dead fish floating by, live fish swimming by, and getting bonked in the head by a cowboy boot and a rusty old license plate.

> For us to have a testimony, we have to first pass the test.

Maybe you've been consumed by something that you're sure will drown you but it's really carrying you toward your destiny. Maybe your fish is that job you hate or that divorce you're going through. Maybe you're in a really dark season.

Tremendous growth comes in the dark and many great journeys have been made at night. Seeds in the ground are in darkness. The Underground Railroad transported hundreds of slaves at night. The children of Israel left Egypt in the dark and a pillar of fire led them (see Exodus 13:18-22). Paul and Silas praised God in the midnight hour and their shackles were broken (see Acts 16:25-26). The womb is dark, but on the other side of darkness there is light—and life begins again.

Tremendous growth comes in the dark and many great journeys have been made at night.

Your whale is transportation to another birthing place, so don't fear the darkness, face it. You've got to face it if you're going to fix it. Even if you have to face it with your eyes closed. In the dark confines of my whale, I just started making fish sandwiches.

You know what's ironic? The same school where I set the lawn on fire, the same school where I was kicked out (George Washington Carver Elementary) now has an annual award called the Rickie G. Rush Outstanding Student award. Every year I go to that school and hand out that award, and I see a plaque on the wall in my honor. It serves as another reminder that when I get discouraged and want to stop fighting, I must continue to come out swinging.

Chapter 13

IT'S TIME TO DANCE

A time to weep, and a time to laugh;
a time to mourn, and a time to
dance (Ecclesiastes 3:4 ESV).

I applaud you for reaching the last chapter. You could have stopped reading at any time, but you didn't. Maybe this book took you a few days or a few months to complete. Maybe you threw it across the room a few times, or maybe you thought, *I wish he was here right now. I'd show him how to keep swinging by landing a few punches to his jaw!* That's okay. You did it—you finished. It means you really are a fighter who's still swinging.

I want to take a minute here and give you one more *What I Really Want You to Remember*, but this time, for the whole book.

Ecclesiastes 3:1-8 says that there are seasons for everything. We'll all face good times and bad times, no exceptions. Some of these seasons cause reactive depression, which is triggered by outward circumstances like loss, emotional fatigue, or physical stress—and it's temporary. Other times we experience clinical depression, which calls for professional help and is treated with therapy and medicine. Many of the negative situations we go through result from the fact that satan hates God, and his way to get back at Him is to hurt us, God's beloved children.

We must discern between God's work and the enemy's work in our lives. God gives us His grace as He allows us to walk through trials to mature us so we can handle blessings; to deepen our relationship with Him; and to make us more Christlike. He is still the Giver of life and all good gifts. Satan is behind all sin and destruction. It's important to know his strategies, recognize him and send him and all of his baggage out of your house saying, "IN THE NAME OF JESUS, GET OUT AND STAY OUT!"

Eight symptoms suggesting depression are: moodiness, changes in appetite and sleep, loss of interest in hobbies, lack of interest in personal appearance, preoccupation with sad thoughts, isolation, and low energy levels. A good cornerman speeds our healing as does our positive self-talk.

Remember, the Bible promises that we will have what we say (see Mark 11:23). The Word, faith, prayer, being under an anointed ministry, the believer's authority, taking every thought captive, a heart of gratitude, and connecting heart to heart with the Lord are necessary to get through this challenging season and walk in the victory that is ordained for you.

GOD CALLS YOU "RIGHTEOUS"

God is so patient with us: *"For though the righteous fall seven times, they rise again"* (Proverbs 24:16). Winning is sometimes no more than refusing to quit. The next time you blow it, remember, you can fail seven times and God still calls you righteous. He never views us as a failure until we give up and quit. Here's a saying that puts it in perspective for me. I hope it's helpful to you, too:

> The wonderful thing about saints is that they were human, they lost their tempers, scolded God, were egotistical or testy or impatient in their turns, made mistakes and regretted them. Still they went on...doggedly blundering toward heaven. —PHYLLIS MCGINLEY

I don't know about you, but I can get up each morning and make a quality commitment to doggedly blunder toward Heaven!

GRACIOUS AND COMPASSIONATE, SLOW TO ANGER, RICH IN LOVE

Failure is not fatal in the healing process. The Bible is full of people who were disgusted by their failures and filled with self-hatred. Don't punish yourself—that's the enemy's job and he's an expert at it. The psalmist promises, *"The Lord is gracious and compassionate, slow to anger and rich in love"* (Psalm 145:8). Many times we're harder on ourselves than God is.

"He has removed our sins as far from us as the east is from the west" (Psalm 103:12 NLT). God has put our sins away to opposite points of the galaxies—light years away where they can no longer affect us at all. Condemnation and wrath are gone; it's as if your

sins had never been committed. They are fully forgiven and never remembered by Him anymore.

No matter what we may feel, we have to quit disqualifying ourselves. God uses those who are weak, flawed, failing, and sinful. Ask yourself, "Who else does He use have?"

We know the names of the following flawed heroes because God told their stories in His book:

- Moses stuttered, but God used him to deliver the Israelites out of Egypt.

- David's armor didn't fit, but he still defeated Goliath.

- Paul rejected John Mark, and they both went on to do great things for God.

- Timothy had ulcers, but he still set up a healthy church.

- Hosea's wife was a prostitute who bore someone else's children, but God still used Hosea to woo the Israelites back to Himself.

- Amos was just a fig farmer, but he powerfully spoke words of social justice, God's omnipotence, and divine judgment.

- Joseph was abused, mistreated, and sold into slavery, but he ascended to second in command, saving both Israel and Egypt during a horrific famine.

- David had an affair with Bathsheba and then arranged for her husband to be killed. But he was still described as a man after God's own heart.

- Jacob lied, cheated, and was insecure, yet he was still one of the patriarchs of Israel.

- Solomon was too rich.

- Jesus was too poor.

- Abraham was too old, yet he was still able to have a child and be the father of a nation.

- David was too young.

- John was self-righteous.

- Samson was co-dependent, slept with a prostitute, and allowed his strength to become his weakness (his long hair).

- Naomi was a widow.

- Moses murdered someone.

- Gideon and Thomas doubted that God had called them.

- Miriam was a gossip.

- Jonah ran from God, was swallowed by a fish, and eventually returned to preach to the Ninevites.

- Jeremiah was depressed all the time.

- Elijah was burned out.

- Martha was controlling worrywart and frustrated that Jesus didn't tell Mary to help out.

- Noah got drunk.

- Peter was afraid of death.

- Habakkuk was impatient.

- Peter had a short fuse, a bad mouth, and denied the Lord three times.

- Zacchaeus was short and unpopular.

- John the Baptist was a little eccentric (he ate locusts and dressed in nothing but camel's hair).

- Lazarus was dead.

God is looking for someone He can use. He is not looking for someone to be perfect, someone who never struggles, or someone who has it all together. He is looking for someone who will depend on Him during his or her time of suffering and depression. For someone who will depend on Him to bring him or her through their valley of the shadow of death. These sound like requirements that I can measure up to—requirements we can all measure up to. It seems to me that God's history is to use anyone who makes him or herself available. He doesn't call the qualified, He qualifies the called.

> He doesn't call the qualified, He qualifies the called.

All of God's giants were weak people. In fact, the Bible says that He chose the weak and foolish people to serve Him so that no one could boast in His sight. Nothing we do qualifies us for God's use, except being foolish and weak:

Take a good look, friends, at who you were when you got called into this life. I don't see many of "the brightest and the best" among you, not many influential, not many from high-society families. Isn't it obvious that God deliberately chose men and women that the culture overlooks and exploits and abuses, chose these "nobodies" to expose the hollow pretensions of the "somebodies"? (1 Corinthians 1:26-28 MSG)

THE PUZZLE

Have you ever tried putting together a 1,000*piece puzzle? The unconnected pieces are like our pendulum swinging. Each day and each circumstance in our lives, good or bad, is a piece of the larger puzzle. As He puts us together, piece by piece, He forms us into the beautiful picture He desires.

Did you know that God loves this process? We get impatient and want it to be over. But He has infinite patience and enjoys watching His kids grow and mature just as an earthly parent delights in coaxing his or her child to crawl, stand up, take the first steps, and ultimately run.

Even with the Scripture and with what God has revealed to us about our destiny, we still don't fully realize what He is doing as He forms us into His masterpiece. I challenge you to look again at the pile of pieces and see what God is doing in your life. By God's grace, we can begin to see ourselves as the picture on the box, each piece connecting with another, until finally we are made whole.

And as you are going through this process of Him carefully putting each piece together, I challenge you to look over the following list and realize that you need to keep on living through each season. Ecclesiastes chapter 1 says that there's a season for everything! I encourage you to:

- keep answering the call
- keep being radical
- keep believing
- keep blessing
- keep calm
- keep competing
- keep creating
- keep dancing
- keep defending
- keep doing your best
- keep driving
- keep exercising
- keep feeding your faith and starving your fears
- keep flourishing
- keep forgiving
- keep getting up again
- keep giving
- keep going
- keep growing
- keep healthy
- keep inspiring
- keep leading
- keep learning
- keep listening
- keep living
- keep loving
- keep motivating
- keep nurturing
- keep obeying
- keep painting
- keep pampering yourself
- keep parenting
- keep participating
- keep planning
- keep playing

- keep plodding
- keep preaching
- keep pursing your dreams
- keep receiving
- keep rejoicing
- keep releasing
- keep remembering
- keep running your race
- keep sharing
- keep shining
- keep shopping
- keep singing
- keep smelling the roses
- keep smiling
- keep sowing and reaping
- keep speaking
- keep standing
- keep striving
- keep studying
- keep swinging
- keep talking
- keep teaching
- keep tithing
- keep trusting
- keep watching
- keep winning
- keep working
- keep worshiping
- keep writing

Circle 10 things on the list that you'll keep doing (or start doing!).

WHO ARE YOU?

Even though we may still be surrounded by some unfavorable circumstances—scattered puzzle pieces—we have to remember that our circumstances are only what we're going through and what we're coming out of—they are *not* who we are. They don't define us. The enemy wants us to focus on what is taking place around us by trying to define who we are by what we're going through. He tries to define the worth of the puzzle by the disordered pieces scattered across the table. *God* is the One who defines who we are and whose we are. And the news is good, good, good!

Second Corinthians 5:21 tells us, *"God made him who had no sin to be sin for us, so that in him we might become the righteousness of God."* Right standing with God has been purchased for us at the cross. We are not merely tolerable, scraping by, or just barely okay—we have been granted the *"righteousness of God."* As our sin was carried and paid for by Him, so His righteousness is given to us. The innocent One was voluntarily punished as if guilty, that we the guilty might be rewarded as if innocent: "Such are we in the sight of God the Father, as is the very Son of God himself."[1]

When God looks at you, He sees you "wearing" the same righteousness as Jesus has. He sees you as a beloved son or daughter, loved as Jesus is loved. (Read this paragraph again, slowly.)

TESTIFY

Contrary to what satan wants us to believe, he is afraid of our finished puzzle—of our connection with God, of our righteousness received as a gift. When God assembles all our pieces, we will have something to say that is going to defeat the enemy. Maybe you've been discouraged because you've had a bad start; but when you tell the story of your rescue and your righteousness, something powerful is going to happen within you and within those who hear it.

When you testify, someone is going to be inspired. *"They triumphed over him by the blood of the Lamb and by the word of their testimony..."* (Revelation 12:11). Every time you testify, you defeat the enemy all over again. Spread the good news that God has not forsaken you or any of His children. Pass this message on to someone else. You, by your very nature, are an encourager, a messenger, and a gift from God. Don't be afraid to share your story—shout it from the housetops.

We used to abuse drugs, abuse alcohol, abuse people, and abuse ourselves. We failed in relationships, failed in school, failed in careers. We've fallen away from people and attempted to fall away from God. But the enemy is still afraid of us because of what God has called us to—His righteousness. God is patiently putting our puzzle together with the fragmented pieces of our lives. And it will be beautiful.

God is patiently putting your puzzle together with the fragmented pieces of your life. And it will be beautiful.

Each of us has an awesome destiny. You have an awesome destiny. Yes, you! Maybe you can't see it yet. Maybe a few of your puzzle pieces have fallen on the floor. That's okay. Make the decision to live one day at a time and fight, always fight. *"Fight the good fight for the faith; take hold of eternal life that you were called to and have made a good confession about in the presence of many witnesses"* (1 Timothy 6:12).[2] Eventually those "one days" will come together to complete your beautiful picture and bring you a victorious future.

God is the One who chose you to be His son or daughter and to bear fruit for His name: *"He is the reason you have a relationship with Christ Jesus, who became for us wisdom from God, and righteousness and sanctification and redemption*" (1 Corinthians 1:30 NET). He has provided everything you need. He knows you intimately. He's the only One who knows your story. He knows you're going to have good days and you're going to have bad days. He wants you to trust Him and come out on the other side of your trial—swinging.

Let me encourage you that if you're down now, you've been down before. If you're crying now, you've cried before. If you're angry now, you've been angry before. If you're alone now, you've been alone before. If you're abandoned now, you've been abandoned before. If you're unemployed now, you've been unemployed before. If you're lacking now, you've been lacking before—but you keep coming back. You've said, "I'm not going to make it" before, you've had people walk away from you before, you have quit before, you've said, "I can't take any more" before—but like the pendulum you are, you keep coming back! If you're being lied to now, you've been lied to before. If you're stepped on now, you've been stepped on before. If you're being walked on now, you've been walked on before. If you're being pronounced dead now, you've been pronounced dead before. If you're being stretched to your limit now, you've been stretched to your limit before—but you kept coming back. Now look at you, you're still swinging.

WHO IS THE PENDULUM?

We've talked an awful lot about pendulums. The question now is not: *what* is the pendulum? Or: where is the pendulum? But: Who is the pendulum? Yes, *who* is the pendulum? As we close, let me propose that the pendulum is you. You have always been the pendulum because you made a decision to keep swinging. This book was written about *you*. Had I told you at the beginning the book was about you, you might have been discouraged, but now you know that you do have courage. You do have strength. You are determined. You are more motivated than you think. You have been hit but you kept moving. You have been down but you're up again. You have been hurt but you're healed.

Here's my departing advice to you: Keep swinging, Pendulum. Keep moving, Pendulum; you are not alone, Pendulum. Someone's depending on you, Pendulum. They're watching you, Pendulum. You're still moving, Pendulum; you're still important, Pendulum, still significant, Pendulum. Still keeping time, Pendulum. You're in good company, Pendulum. God has never left you, Pendulum. He has never forsaken you, Pendulum. It doesn't mean you won't stop, Pendulum; it *does* mean you can restart, Pendulum. You still have a purpose, Pendulum; you are still living, Pendulum. Come out swinging, Pendulum. You may not like where you are, Pendulum, but this book has been sent to you to remind you, Pendulum, that time has been keeping up with you, Pendulum. And wherever you are in your life, Pendulum, you are right on time. And until I see you next round—swing, Pendulum, swing!

ENDNOTES

1. Jamieson, Fausset, and Brown Commentary, "Bible Tools: 2 Corinthians 5:21," Church of the Great God, http://www.bibletools.org/index.cfm/fuseaction/Bible.show/sVerseID/28899/eVerseID/28899/RTD/jfb (accessed 8/15/14).

2. *Holman Christian Standard Bible.*

Tear out this page and put it some place you will see it daily to remind you that no matter what, God can use you!

GOD DOES NOT CALL THE QUALIFIED, HE QUALIFIES THE CALLED

- Moses stuttered, but God used him to deliver the Israelites out of Egypt.

- David's armor didn't fit but he still defeated Goliath.

- Paul rejected John Mark and they both went on to do great things for God.

- Timothy had ulcers, but he still set up a healthy church.

- Hosea's wife was a prostitute who bore someone else's children, but God still used Hosea to woo the Israelites back to Himself.

- Amos was just a fig farmer but powerfully spoke words of social justice, God's omnipotence, and divine judgment.

- Joseph was abused, mistreated, and sold into slavery, but ascended to second in command, saving both Israel and Egypt during a horrific famine.

- David had an affair with Bathsheba and then arranged for her husband to be killed. But he was still described as a man after God's own heart.

- Jacob lied, cheated, and was insecure, yet he was still one of the patriarchs of Israel.

- Solomon was too rich.

- Jesus was too poor.
- Abraham was too old, yet he was still able to have a child and be the father of a nation.
- David was too young.
- John was self-righteous.
- Samson was co-dependent, slept with a prostitute and allowed his strength to become his weakness (his long hair).
- Naomi was a widow.
- Moses murdered someone.
- Gideon and Thomas doubted that God had called them.
- Miriam was a gossip.
- Jonah ran from God, was swallowed by a fish, and eventually returned to preach to the Ninevites.
- Jeremiah was depressed all the time.
- Elijah was burned out.
- Martha was a worrywart.
- Martha was controlling and frustrated that Jesus didn't tell Mary to help out.
- Noah got drunk.
- Peter was afraid of death.
- Habakkuk was impatient.
- Peter had a short fuse, a bad mouth, and denied the Lord three times.
- Zacchaeus was short and unpopular.
- John the Baptist was a little eccentric (he ate locusts and dressed in nothing but camel's hair).
- Lazarus was dead.

ABOUT RICKIE G. RUSH

Rickie G. Rush is the pastor of one of the most progressive, flourishing ministries in the United States. He is a gifted pastor and teacher who communicates God's Word with excellence and simplicity, under the anointing of the Holy Spirit.

Pastor Rush prayed for God's enablement to preach to the world and his territory has certainly been enlarged. His Spirit-filled book ministry has caused the lives of many to be enriched, illuminated, and forever changed.

Pastor Rush writes under the inspiration of God and can relate to the issues of the average person. His upbringing coupled with early losses in life have all worked together to make him reachable and touchable to the masses—to the world! His aim is to imitate Christ and see others as they can be, not just as they are.

Contact Information
Inspiring Body of Christ Church
7701 S. Westmoreland Road
Dallas, TX 75237
Phone: 972-572-4262
Website: ibocchurch.org
www.RICKIERUSH.com

OTHER BOOKS BY RICKIE G. RUSH

May I Have Your Order, Please?